Reconstructing Racial Identity and the African Past
in the Dominican Republic

New World Diasporas

D1595677

UNIVERSITY PRESS OF FLORIDA

Florida A&M University, Tallahassee
Florida Atlantic University, Boca Raton
Florida Gulf Coast University, Ft. Myers
Florida International University, Miami
Florida State University, Tallahassee
New College of Florida, Sarasota
University of Central Florida, Orlando
University of Florida, Gainesville
University of North Florida, Jacksonville
University of South Florida, Tampa
University of West Florida, Pensacola

Reconstructing Racial Identity and the African Past in the Dominican Republic

Kimberly Eison Simmons

University Press of Florida
Gainesville/Tallahassee/Tampa/Boca Raton
Pensacola/Orlando/Miami/Jacksonville/Ft. Myers/Sarasota

15   14   13   12   11   10   6   5   4   3   2   1

First cloth printing, 2009
First paperback printing, 2010

Library of Congress Cataloging-in-Publication Data
Simmons, Kimberly Eison.
Reconstructing racial identity and the African past in the Dominican
Republic / Kimberly Eison Simmons.
p. cm. — (New World diasporas)
Includes bibliographical references and index.
ISBN 978-0-8130-3374-7 (cloth)
ISBN 978-0-8130-3675-5 (paper)
1. Blacks—Race identity—Dominican Republic. 2. Ethnicity—Dominican
Republic. 3. National characteristics, Dominican. I. Title.
F1941.B55S56 2009
305.896'07293—dc22   2009001974

The University Press of Florida is the scholarly publishing agency for the
State University System of Florida, comprising Florida A&M Univer-
sity, Florida Atlantic University, Florida Gulf Coast University, Florida
International University, Florida State University, New College of Florida,
University of Central Florida, University of Florida, University of North
Florida, University of South Florida, and University of West Florida.

University Press of Florida
15 Northwest 15th Street
Gainesville, FL 32611-2079
www.upf.com

For my children,
Asha, Aria, and Aidan,
my husband and colleague,
David S. Simmons,
my parents,
Ludia and Wilson Eison, Jr.,
and my sister and her family,
Kamika, Bobby, Sean, Chris, and Brandon
with love and gratitude

Contents

Illustrations

Appendixes

Acknowledgments

Anyone who knows me knows that this book project is near and dear to me. I first went to the Dominican Republic in 1993 as a student. It was the first of several research experiences in the country, and I lived and worked there from 2000 to 2004. Two of my children were born in the Dominican Republic (and have dual citizenship), and my oldest daughter attended an international school there through first grade. Without doubt, the Dominican Republic is a very special place to my family. At one point in time we called the Dominican Republic "home," and our children claim "Dominican," in addition to "American" as a part of their experience and heritage. As a student, researcher, mother, wife, colleague, neighbor, friend, *co-madre*, and now professor, I straddled the Dominican Republic and the United States. I learned a great deal over time, and I am truly grateful for all of the support that I have received over the years as my family and I were incorporated into Dominican life and community. I would like to take this opportunity to thank the many people who helped to make this book possible.

Several of my colleagues at the University of South Carolina offered support and advice as I approached the book project. I thank all of my colleagues in the Department of Anthropology and the African American Studies Program, especially Ann Kingsolver, Tom Leatherman, Karl Heider, Alice Kasakoff, David Simmons, Terry Weik, Jennifer Reynolds, Marc Moskowitz, Todd Shaw, Bobby Donaldson, Andrew Billingsley, Kent Germany, Stephanie Mitchem, Valinda Littlefield, Dan Littlefield, and Cleveland Sellers. Thanks go to Catherine Keegan, Claudia Carriere, Valerie Ashford, and Carolyn Sutton (administrative assistants) for their assistance over the past couple of years. Thanks also go to my colleagues in the Women's and Gender Studies Program and Latin American, Caribbean, and Latino/a Studies. I would also like to thank the dean of the College of Arts and Sciences, Dr. Mary Anne Fitzpatrick, for her ongoing support.

I have been a part of different cohorts over the years. The African Diaspora Research Project (ADRP) at Michigan State University (MSU) was a place where many of us grew intellectually under the direction of the late Ruth Simms Hamilton. I would like to thank my ADRP colleagues, Edward Paulino, Chege Githoria, Mtafiti Imara, Noel Allende-Goita, Ramond Familusi, Michael Hanson, and Joan Reid, the project secretary. Dr. Ruth Simms

Hamilton was a professor and mentor, and she had a profound effect on me in terms of my interest in the African diaspora. I would also like to thank Scott Whiteford, Laurie Medina, Judy Pugh, and Ann Millard at MSU for their support and feedback on my early work when I was in graduate school. Along these lines, I also thank Mike Whiteford and Huang Shu-min at Iowa State University, where I first developed an interest in conducting research in the Dominican Republic.

I would like to thank my colleagues in the Dominican Republic, from the Council on International Educational Exchange (CIEE/Council Study Center), La Pontificia Universidad Católica Madre y Maestra (PUCMM), and several women's organizations. Special thanks go to Carmen Luisa González, Thelma Román, María Filomena González, Rubén Silie, Nancy Bisonó, Liliana Montenegro, Federica Castro, Ana Margarita Hache, Rafael Yunén, Luis Felipe Rodríguez, Carlos Fernández Rocha, Blas Jiménez, Carlos Andújar, Yngris Balbuena, Tanya Serrata, Francis Nuñez, Mariana Moreno, Susi Pola, Ochy Curiel, Melba González, Elaine Acacio, Marcos Polo, Rich Weber, Sarah Ross, Nathaniel Thompson, Lynne Guitar, Rafael Cerda, Hector Garcia, and Eduardo Capellán. I thank the members of Identidad de las Mujeres Afro in the Dominican Republic, the participants of the focus groups, and everyone I interviewed. I thank our neighbors in Santiago as well as our friends, many of whom have become extended family. Special thanks go to Carmen Luisa González and her family (abuela, Lillybeth, Laura, and Jolly), Nancy Bisonó and her family (Dionisio, Dionisio Alberto, and Leonardo), Melba González and her family (Emilio, Molly, and Ramon), Elaine and Marcos Polo and their family (Portia and Mekhi), and Carmen Ligia Duarte for the very important work of helping to take care of my children. I would also like to thank my CIEE colleagues in the United States, especially Christine Wintersteen, Catherine Scruggs, and Eero Jesurun. It was because of CIEE that I returned to the Dominican Republic in 2000 to live and work.

I have given numerous conference papers over the years on my research in the Dominican Republic and have received tremendous support and feedback from several people. I would like to thank all of my "cheerleaders," especially Faye V. Harrison, Lee Baker, Karla Slocum, Kia Caldwell, Bayo Holsey, Raquel Capeda, Rachel Afi Quinn, Charles Price, Bernd Reiter, Chuck Haney, Louise Rowe, Deborah Thomas, John Jackson, A. Lynn Bolles, Irma McClaurin, Michael Blakey, Cheryl Rodriguez, Dana-ain Davis, Kevin Foster, Robert Adams, Marla Frederick, Janis Hutchinson, Pem Buck, Gina Perez, Gina Sanchez Gibau, Isar Godreau, Raymond Codrington, Elizabeth Chin, Tracey Weldon, Qiana Whitted, Tracy Montague, Amy Streets, Valesta

Wiggins, Erica Gibson, Drucilla Barker, Charles Cobb, Hilary Jones, Mark Whitaker, Clare Barrington, Rosalind Johnson, David Wilson, Dawn-Elissa Fischer, Elise Ahyi, Natalie Washington-Weik, Jemima Pierre, Marc Perry, Marvin McAllister, Toni Tildon, Rheeda Walker-Obasi, Sybil Rosado, Yarimar Bonilla, Joanna Casey, Yvonne Rodgers, Candace Romero, Clarissa Bennett, Rosario Espinal, Lynn Weber, Kenneth Kelly, Chandana Kulkarni and family, Jennette Davis and family, and Kesho Scott, and Helen Safa. Along these lines, I would like to thank my colleagues in the Association of Black Anthropologists (ABA), the Association for Feminist Anthropology (AFA), the Latin American Studies Association (LASA), the Caribbean Studies Association (CSA), and the Association for the Study of the Worldwide African Diaspora (ASWAD). In addition, I thank some of my fellow Dominicanists—Denise Brennan, Ginetta Candelario, Robin Derby, April Mayes, Ana Aparicio, Carlos Decena, Zaire Dinzey, and Edward Paulino—for their support and for ongoing conversations about what is of interest to all of us.

I have been fortunate to have worked with several people over the past couple of years to make this project a reality. I thank Stacy Lathrop for assisting me with editing during the early writing of the book. I offer my sincerest thanks to Kimberly Cavanagh, my doctoral student, for her invaluable assistance over the past year with editing, formatting, and proofreading. I also thank Karma Frierson for her editorial assistance with the manuscript in the summer of 2007 and Christine Sweeney for copyediting the book.

I am very excited about this book being a part of Kevin Yelvington's book series, New World Diasporas, with the University Press of Florida (UPF). I would like to thank Kevin for his tremendous support over the past couple of years as well as Eli Bortz, Heather R. Turci, and Susan Albury at the UPF for their enthusiastic support of me and the book project. I would also like to thank the anonymous reviewers for their insightful comments and suggestions.

I have published two articles, one book chapter, and an essay based on this work and would like to thank the different publishers for giving me permission to use them in this book. I especially thank Rutgers University Press for giving me permission to use my book chapter "A Passion for Sameness: Encountering a Black Feminist Self in Fieldwork in the Dominican Republic," which was published in 2001 in *Black Feminist Anthropology: Theory, Praxis, Politics, and Poetics*, edited by Irma Mcclaurin. Thanks also go to Blackwell Publishing for permission to use my works: my essay "Racial Enculturation and Lived Experience: Reflections on Race at Home and Abroad," *Anthropology News* 47(2) (2006): 10–11; and my article "Navigating the Racial Terrain: Blackness and Mixedness in the United States and the Dominican Republic,"

Transforming Anthropology 16(2): 95–111. Finally, thanks go to Lexington Books for permission to use my article "*Somos una Liga: Afro-Dominicanidad* and the Articulation of New Racial Identities in the Dominican Republic," *Wadabagei: A Journal of the Caribbean and Its Diaspora* 8(1) (2005): 51–64.

In addition to all of my colleagues, I would like to thank all of my students over the years, on the CIEE program and at the University of South Carolina, for their feedback and discussions surrounding racial identity in the Dominican Republic, the United States, and throughout the African diaspora. We have had many spirited discussions over the past few semesters. I would also like to extend a word of thanks to my neighbors—everyone knew I had a book to write and they were supportive in many ways. Among others, special thanks go to Michelle Miller and her family (Pamela Brackett and Nola Miller), Carlos and Faith Hart and their family (Zac and Zar), Ivonne Bailey, Jonathan Guzman and family (Stanley and Lucia), Jerry and Jackie Mays, Stanley and Sylvia Montgomery, and Jackie and Manuel Diaz and their family.

My family has been very supportive and encouraging over the years in words and deeds. I would like to offer a special thanks to my parents, Ludia and Wilson Eison; my sister, Kamika Eison Wheatley, and her family (Bobby, Sean, Chris, and Brandon); my uncle Boyce Rowe; my aunt Benja Waugh; my aunt Lela Haynes and family (Carolyn, Robert, and Brian); my aunt Rebecca Hill and family (Gene, Damon, Jason, and Sean); Kermit Parsons and his family; my aunt Jeannette Davis and family; and my extended family in Tennessee, Indiana, Illinois, and around the United States. I also thank my in-laws, Jim and Judi Simmons, Rick, Audrey, Aaron, Jeremy, and Phyllis Jones. Thanks to all of you for your prayers and positive thoughts. Finally, I would like to offer my sincerest thanks to my family—to David (my husband and colleague) and our children, Asha, Aria, and Aidan—for their love, support, and encouragement as I worked to complete this book. Thank you all—I love you all very much.

To all of you, and many more, I am truly grateful.

Introduction
Burying the African Past

We have not been able to grasp our negritude yet.

Blas Jiménez, *Mirrors of the Heart*

The Signos de Identidad (Signs of Identity) exhibit is inside the Sala de Antropología (Anthropology Room), at the Centro Cultural Eduardo León Jimenes in Santiago de los Caballeros, Dominican Republic, and it displays artifacts and representations of Dominican people and culture. In a large room with three exhibits dedicated to the Spanish, Taínos, and Africans respectively, Signos de Identidad reflects the heart of the Dominican *liga* (mixture) in folklore, concepts of identity, and nation. Visitors can stand in front of both the Spanish and Taíno exhibits, look directly into the cases, and read about the artifacts and contributions of both of these groups to Dominican life and culture. The African exhibit is different, however. At a glance, it looks like an enclosed wall with several lighted rectangular openings. It is not until you look inside one of the openings that the significance of the exhibit is made clear. Each opening is a window into the African past and present in terms of cultural contributions to Dominican life, culture, and peoplehood. From drums and colorful fabric to musical forms and foods, the exhibit is a powerful display not only because it points to Africa and Africans' historic contribution but also because it signifies the buried nature of the African past in Dominican memory and identity.

Recently, there has been much discussion of black denial associated with Dominicans (Candelario 2007) in terms of how they define themselves without seemingly taking their African ancestry into account. On June 13, 2007, the *Miami Herald* published an article in its special series on Afro–Latin Americans; the article by Frances Robles on the Dominican Republic was entitled "Black Denial."[1] I was interviewed for this story, but none of the interview was used for the piece. I suspect this was, in part, because I problematized denial and what it means to *deny* African heritage. While Dominicans use popular expressions like "black behind the ear" (Candelario 2007, 2001), implying a hidden or concealed nature of African ancestry, denial is different. The word "denial" suggests that there is a negative response to a question or idea. In other words, "denial" implies that Dominicans do not believe that they *have* African ancestry. And this is not the case. To the contrary, African ancestry is often acknowledged, but it is downplayed and relegated to a place that is hidden or "behind the ear" as the saying goes. In 1993, the Dominican-born acclaimed writer Julia Alvarez wrote about her personal experiences with color in the Dominican Republic in *Essence*, a magazine with a predominantly African American women's audience. She talked about how blackness—to be black—is something that Dominicans have hidden "behind the ear," again suggesting the concurrent presence and concealed nature of blackness (Candelario 2007).

An example often given for black denial is that of the hair-straightening practice in the Dominican Republic, but this is not unique to Dominicans— it is also the experience of African Americans (Craig 2002; Rooks 1996) and other women throughout the African diaspora as they have also internalized similar ideals of beauty, a "light, near white" ideal, and what is socially appropriate in terms of hairstyles. As with Dominican women, presentation of self is very important among African American women. This is especially the case of middle-class African Americans in which to have your hair "done" is to have it straightened. I was used to the social pressures surrounding hair before I left for the Dominican Republic, so when I encountered it, it was something familiar to me.

By the time I left for the Dominican Republic the first time in 1993, I was wearing my hair in a naturally curly style. I *discovered* that I could wear my hair this way when I was in college. Before then, I always *did* my hair. This meant roller setting my hair or using a curling or flat iron for a straight style with a loose curl. Social pressures are strong in the African American community—especially among those in the middle class—for a particular hairstyle. Growing up, I was used to seeing women in my family get their hair done either at a salon or at home. I would often accompany them to the salon. This was part of how they presented themselves when they went out in public, on special occasions, and for important events. My mother or grandmother often straightened my hair, but when I got older, I either went to a salon or did it myself. When I went to college, I was armed with everything I needed to do my hair especially since I was going to a predominantly white college in a predominantly white town. In my experience, white stylists did—and do not—like to straighten my hair. I've heard comments like "women pay a lot of money to have curls like yours. Why do you want to straighten you hair?" One day, I was running late and didn't get to dry and straighten my hair, and as it dried naturally, I realized that it *looked fine*, and I liked it. As a result, I started wearing it curly, and I as began my own process of reflection, thinking about the politics of hair in the African American community, I made a conscious decision to wear my hair that way, in a "natural" style.

When I went home for the first time with curly hair, my mother, not used to seeing my hair styled that way, said "What are you going to do with your hair?" and I said, "It's done." While I remember seeing women in my family get their hair straightened, I also remember seeing my mother wear her hair in an afro in the 1970s like other women during the time. When I was in first grade, I wanted an afro like the other black girls in my school. I had two long braids (pigtails as they were called), and people often thought I was Latina. I went home and asked my mother if I could have an afro like the other girls. "I'm not going to cut your hair," my mother said. So, she bought a brown afro wig for me to wear to school. I was happy. Friends—used to seeing my hair in one way—were curious about my new hairstyle. I only told my closest friends that it was a wig. My time with the wig was short-lived, however, as one day during recess, a strong wind carried my wig across the playground. I decided from that point forward that I would just wear my hair in two braids and answer questions about "what I was." So, while social forces were at play (from straightening hair, wearing an afro, and back to straightening hair), I also witnessed and experienced women going against the social grain, aware of the social pressures and the politics. Today, while I tend to wear my hair curly most of the time, I still straighten my hair on different occasions, but I am always aware of the politics surrounding hair and the fact that I can *choose* to wear my hair curly *or* straight.

In the African American community, curly hair represents mixture (either historic mixture or more recent mixture in families) and signifies having European and/or Native American ancestry. A hair care product called Mixed Chicks is marketed toward women with naturally curly hair. I learned about the product after a friend gave me a postcard flyer with the product information and suggested that I might want to try it. The following statement is taken from the company's website (www.mixedchicks.net): "finally, a curl-defining system designed for 'us.' whether [*sic*] you're black, white, asian [*sic*], latin [*sic*], Mediterranean, or any glorious combination of the above, you'll love the way these non-sticky, lightweight, products leave your hair inviting to touch as they define and lock moisture into every curl." Not only does curly hair signify mixedness in the African American community, it often connotes having what is known as "good hair." I grew up hearing that I had "good hair." All around me, from friends, strangers, family members, hair stylists, and others, I carried that label. Today, my daughters, now twelve and seven, hear the same sentiment as people make comments about their hair. The opposite of good hair is bad hair, which implies having "kinky," tightly curled, or what some would refer to as "nappy" hair (a racially charged term that is very offensive). Good hair and bad hair are ways of talking about texture and appearance of hair while connoting signs of blackness, whiteness, and mixedness. I was used to this type of categorization when I left for the Dominican Republic. As Candelario (2007) points out, good hair (*pelo bueno*) and bad hair (*pelo malo*) continue to be ways that Dominican women talk about and describe hair. Women with "bad hair" as well as "good hair" may chose to chemically relax their hair for manageability and for social reasons. Hair relaxers provide a way for some women to straighten their hair and maintain the style despite climate and humidity. The politics of hair is just one of the several parallel examples and experiences between Dominicans and African Americans. Another is the politics of skin color and colorization (intra-group naming practices).

Most often African Americans use light-, brown-, and dark-skinned to refer to skin color variation (Simmons 2008). The Dominican counterpart to light-skinned is *indio claro*, and dark-skinned is *indio oscuro*. I discuss *indio* as a construction and in historical and social context in chapter 2. There are other common color terms used among both Dominicans and African Americans to describe color, but these are the most prevalent descriptors. So while the United States is usually described as having black-white bipolar racial politics (which is true), the intra-group colorization practice among African Americans is very similar to that of Dominicans.

Returning to the point of black denial in the Dominican Republic, with regard to Africa, the question remains, what have Dominicans learned, and not learned, about Africa, the African presence on the island, and its contribution to Dominican culture and peoplehood? What is reinforced in schools, families, and other social institutions? As I discuss later in the book, Dominicans' historical construction of blackness used Haiti and Haitians as a point of reference of not only what it meant to be black but also of African descent. Dominicans defined themselves as mixed in relation to Haitians, whom they defined as black. Unpacking the term black in the Dominican Republic evokes an African past, dark skin color, poverty, and other negative associations. In a relational sense, Dominican mixedness is constructed vis-à-vis Haitian blackness, but this meaning shifts in the United States because of the situated meaning of blackness. Blackness, once understood within the context of Hispaniola, is called into question as many Dominicans are considered to be black in the context of the United States. Importantly, there is an epistemological shift in blackness as Dominicans encounter African

Figure I.1. Map of Hispaniola.

Americans—who look like them—and are defined, and define themselves, as black.

On the surface, while it may seem that Dominicans assert black denial, I argue that blackness was actually denied Dominican people for much of the twentieth century by the state in efforts to whiten the population as witnessed by immigration policies, national racial and color categories, and other socialization practices where mixture was promoted over blackness. For this reason, the idea of being black, of having African ancestry and embodying this in terms of identity and racial and color categories, is not usually expressed by Dominicans in terms of how they identify themselves. This is changing, however.

My Arrival Story

My own personal experiences with race, color, and nationality led me to pursue questions of race and identity in Dominican Republic through an anthropological perspective. Since childhood, questions like "what are you?"

and "are you mixed?" prompted me to explain my own history and ancestry to complete strangers on a regular basis. For as long as I can remember, I have been both black and light-skinned.[2] I understood black to be a larger umbrella term for a particular community of people with a history and experience in the United States. The other label (light-skinned) was one used within the black community to talk about color and experience.

When I began graduate work in anthropology, I wanted to focus on race, color, gender, and identity in the African diaspora with an emphasis on the Hispanic Caribbean. I became familiar with the Dominican Republic when I was exploring study abroad programs in college. As I read more about Dominican history and culture, I learned about the country's color classification system and noticed some similarities with respect to African Americans. My research in the Dominican Republic has been longitudinal, beginning in 1993. I worked closely with Carmen Luisa "Lilly" González, who was the director of the Women's Studies Program at the Pontificia Universidad Católica Madre y Maestra (PUCMM) in Santiago at the time. Lilly was very instrumental in helping me make contacts with women's organizations in both Santiago and Santo Domingo. Over the years, Lilly and I have become close friends, colleagues, and co-madres, and her assistance was invaluable over the years.

After 1993, I conducted a pilot study and dissertation research and continued to do follow-up research until the present. From 2000 to 2004, I lived and worked in Santiago, where I directed a study abroad program in Spanish language and Caribbean studies through the Council on International Educational Exchange (CIEE Study Center) at the PUCMM. During this time, I had the opportunity to work with college students from different colleges and universities in the United States, to work and collaborate with Dominican colleagues at the PUCMM and in Santo Domingo, and to participate in workshops and meetings on topics of race, gender, and identity in the country. Four years of living and working in the Dominican Republic provided me with a unique opportunity to experience life much like my counterparts at the PUCMM. Through faculty meetings, having children in elementary school and preschool, attending meetings with neighbors about issues with the apartment building, and other day-to-day experiences, I had a more in-depth understanding about life, identity, and experience in the Dominican Republic.

My husband, David, was completing his post-doctoral work at the time. He also later directed the CIEE summer program in community health and served as a resident director of the semester program when I was on maternity leave. Asha, our oldest daughter, went through first grade at a bilingual international school in Santiago with majority instruction in Spanish. When we returned to the United States in 2004 to work at the University of South Carolina, Asha was considered an ESOL student and was considered a Latina student from the Dominican Republic. Aria and Aidan, our younger two children, were born in the Dominican Republic and have dual citizenship with U.S. and Dominican passports as per U.S. embassy regulations. (According to documentation provided by the U.S. embassy in Santo Domingo, children born of U.S. citizens in the Dominican Republic were required to obtain a Dominican passport to establish place of birth before applying for a U.S. passport and U.S. citizenship [record of birth abroad].) As a family, we grew to call the Dominican Republic home and were gradually incorporated into Dominican society over time with colleagues, friends, and fictive kin and extended family. Like many of our middle-class counterparts, we attended weddings, celebrations, Christmas gatherings, outings, and went on occasional weekend vacations to the coast. Much like Kondo's experience in Japan (Kondo 1990), I soon realized that there was a Dominicanization process taking place, and I had become Dominicanized (a statement often made by Dominicans as well as Americans) because of my gradual incorporation. Ever the "light-skinned black woman" and anthropologist from the United States, I became a part of a process that I was researching, only in reverse.

While I was used to being defined and defining myself as light-skinned, I was not used to the idea of *being* mulatto (or *india*, another specific term connoting mixture). Luis, a close friend, said to me, "You are *mulata* here," and I remember how I *felt* when he made the comment, but over time I understood that is how I was *viewed*—as *mulata*, *india*, or simply as mixed. I contemplated what it meant to be *mulata* in the Dominican Republic and black in the United States. I then wondered what it was like for Dominicans to be *indio* or *mulato* in the Dominican Republic and black in the United States. Embracing an identity that does not reflect a sense of one's self is not a seamless process; it takes time and requires that one step back and ask why this is the way it is.

I remember when Luis invited me over for lunch for the first time. His mother is Argentinean, and his father is Dominican, and Luis and his siblings grew up with a sense of being *mulato* unlike other Dominicans (who are understood as being mixed but with reference to *indio*). Their parents told them that they were *mulato*, and he defined himself that way. When Luis introduced me to his father, his father looked at me and said, "Tú no eres gringa gringa . . . tú tienes la sangre" (you are not a gringa gringa [American] . . . you have the blood." He then said, "You are like Luis." Knowing what he meant, I said, "Yes, this is true . . . I have the blood." In this case, blood meant African ancestry.

Luis's mother, Susi, is a part of an ongoing feminist movement in the Dominican Republic and writes a newspaper column challenging *machismo* in Dominican society. At the time, Susi was the director of the Nucleo de Apoyo a la Mujer (Nucleus of Support for Women) in Santiago. This was a center that provided support to women experiencing domestic abuse or needing assistance with legal issues. Susi hosted a weekly television program called *Mujer Hoy* (Today's Woman) and discussed various topics on women's rights, health, and other issues. She invited me on the show to talk about racial identity. Before the program aired, one of her reporters interviewed people around the city about race and color. When the reporter asked if Dominicans were racist, many of the people responded that they were— toward Haitians. When the reporter asked if a dark-skinned woman was *negra* (black), she replied, "No soy negra, soy chocolate" (I am not black, I am chocolate). Susi and I discussed the responses and the issue of race and color during the program and the issue of blackness in particular.

One of my colleagues at the PUCMM, who is also from Argentina, commented to me one day that it must be difficult for me, as an American, to live in the Dominican Republic. "Aqui es fundamentalmente Africano" (here it is fundamentally African). She was referring to a lack of punctuality in terms of meetings and events starting late, the social importance of greetings, and the prolonged process of accomplishing everyday tasks. I told her that as an African American I was actually very familiar with it as there are similar patterns of greetings and approaches to time among African Americans. She also commented that Dominicans often think that the Dominican Republic is like Spain and it is not; "It is like Africa," she said. When meetings were scheduled, people would often ask "la hora Dominicana" (Dominican time) or "la hora Americana" (American time). American time meant that the meeting would start on time and that people should arrive a little before then so as to be ready to start. Dominican time allowed for more flexibility with the meeting starting a little later than scheduled. African Americans refer to this as "CP time" (colored people's time).

My growing understanding of this complex topic is from living, working, and conducting research—with interviews, focus groups, and archival research—in Santiago over time. Many of the observations are based on everyday interactions, conversations, and reflections based on print and television media. Dominicans often asked me if I was born "there" (United States) and if my parents were born "here" (Dominican Republic). Questions about my family and me turned into conversations and interviews that provided an avenue to talk about Dominican experience "here" and "there" as well as racial identity. In 1998, my husband, David, our daughter, Asha, and I went to Puerto Plata (a coastal community). The hotel had only recently opened but already had a number of tourists from Germany and Canada. On this particular weekend, there were a few Dominicans there as well—from the Dominican Republic and from the United States. I soon learned that there was the expectation that Dominicans should speak Spanish when interacting with the local hotel staff. This was evident as we witnessed a number of exchanges between staff and hotel guests. When members of the hotel staff interacted with European guests, they attempted to speak German or English. However, the language of choice by the hotel staff was Spanish, even with Dominican guests who spoke English more than Spanish. When David went to get a towel, the attendant only spoke to him in Spanish. David explained that he was learning Spanish and wasn't fluent, at which point the attendant told him to be proud of being Dominican and speak Spanish—so they continued in Spanish. When David walked away, he overhead the same attendant speaking fluent English to a Canadian guest. We had similar experiences over the years as we were considered to be Dominican by hotel staff. More recently, on a trip to the Dominican Republic in the summer of 2008, we spent four days in Puerto Plata with our children and our goddaughter, who lives in Santiago. There seemed to be as many Dominicans (from the Dominican Republic and the United States) there during those days as European and white American guests. As we greeted one of the staff attendants, he said, "You are Dominican, right? With that color, you have to be Dominican."

We continued having similar experiences over time. The issue of being "Dominican" versus "Dominican Dominican" emerged as a way of describing Dominicans born here (Dominican Republic) versus there (United States). "Dominican Dominican" translated into a type of "authenticity." Those born in the United States or residing there for several years were considered "Dominican," but those who were born in the Dominican Republic, and lived and resided in the Dominican Republic, were considered "Dominican Dominican." It was something about the experience of never leaving, or leaving temporarily but continuing to reside in, the Dominican Republic that meant that one was "truly" Dominican. "Dominican Dominican" claimed a more "authentic" identity, history, and experience.

Black in the Dominican Republic and the United States

Again, the popular saying "black behind the ears" is manifested in many ways in the Dominican Republic. While Dominicans do not readily define themselves as black, they use "black" in everyday discourse to define or talk about other people. During a conversation, it is common to hear someone refer to someone else as "negro" or "negra" and it has nothing to do with color. In this way, "negro" is very similar to the usage of the n-word among African Americans to connote a history, connection, and relationship between people. During my first trip to the Dominican Republic, I met an older woman who was referred to by others as "Doña Negra." She later told me that she considered herself to be black because she was dark-skinned, and that it was a term of endearment. Someone can be called "negro" without being dark-skinned. It is common to have someone in the family who is known as "negro" and addressed that way in conversations. Some of our close friends invited us over for dinner for a family gathering. As one of the uncles engaged in conversation with someone else, someone wanting his attention said "negro . . . ," and he turned around to respond as if his name had been called. While *negro/a* can be—and is—a term of endearment among Dominicans, it is also a word often used to describe Haitians with negative connotations. It can also take on more of the characteristics of the n-word because of the influence of American rap music in the Dominican Republic.

While the term *negro/a* circulates in Dominican life, society, and practice, Dominicans typically do not define themselves in this way. Largely, many people do not accept this label easily because of its historical and sociocultural significance in the Dominican Republic. The African American students I worked with on the CIEE program often had a difficult time understanding race and what seemed to be a denial of blackness in the Dominican Republic. The students often commented that when Dominicans "deny" that they are black, they are denying "who they are" and are not proud of being black. "All they have to do is look in the mirror," one student told me. "How can they deny they are black?" Like other identities, racial identities are constructed, learned, and internalized. Despite the fact that identities are fluid and changing, there is a sense that they are fixed (Simmons 2006). This means that because of racial socialization, people have a sense of *who they are* in racial terms rooted in history, place, and experience. In other words, black students often said that they could not *stop being black*, that they would *always be black*. For the students, being black was a fixed identity even though they understood—intellectually speaking—that identities were fluid. What I tried to get them to see was that while they *were black*, some of them were not perceived as black in the Dominican Republic because of racial politics and racialization.

I reminded students of the collective naming processes throughout the African American experience (Negro, colored, Afro-American, black, African American) as a way of addressing fluidity of categories. All of these categories have been used at different points in time in history to refer to the same group of people and their descendants. Even though the group name has changed over time, people do not always identify in the same way or easily accept the change. Even though African American was the "official" term during the 1980s and 1990s, some of the students said that they still preferred to define themselves as black even though they knew that the term "African American" referred to them (on applications, for example).

I remember when the shift from black to African American occurred in the late 1980s. I was in college. I was in a store one day when a white woman stopped and asked me, "What are you?" When I responded "I'm African American," a chill came over me—literally—as this was the first time that I had used the term to define myself. Until that time, I always used "black" to describe myself, and it *felt different* to use another category that was supposed to just replace the other. I was majoring in what was then "Afro-American Studies," which soon became "African American Studies." All around, "black" seem to change to "African American" except in the case of established groups and organizations like the Black Cultural Center and the Young, Gifted, and Black Gospel Choir on campus. Over time, I grew to be more comfortable with the term, but part of me still continued to identify as black. During the time of the black to African American transition, I went to Tennessee to visit my family. I remember telling my great-grandfather, a former sharecropper turned landowner, that "we were calling ourselves African American now," to which he responded, "I do not care what you call yourself; I am Colored." Reflecting on what he said much later made sense to me because of his situated and lived racial experience in the South.

As I discuss later in the book, this is something that Dominicans not only faced in the Dominican Republic but also in the United States. In 1998 in the Dominican Republic, a new color category—*mulato*—was introduced on the *cédula* (the national identification card) and was supposed to (according to media reports and information by state officials) replace *indio*. This did not happen, however, as both remained as color categories, and officials were left with two choices representing mixture. In the United States, blackness—and the category "black"—takes on new meaning as Dominicans often find themselves being defined by other people as black. A friend and colleague, Edward Paulino, told me about an experience he had in Washington, D.C. when he lived and worked there. At that time, Edward was used to taking the bus, and the bus driver, an African American man, would often greet him with an upward nod of the head while saying "What's up?" In turn, Edward responded to the man and later realized the driver was "claiming" him (as an African American) since this is often a greeting among African American men.

In these examples, context is important as is how people see themselves connected to place and other people while having a sense of themselves. While there may be fluidity of categories, people interact with these categories differently (accepting them in certain contexts or rejecting them). For people who understand that the context has changed (as in the case of African Americans in the Dominican Republic or Dominicans in the United States), the process of reconstructing racial identity is often a gradual one as they interact with new definitions, laws, and people who define them in new and different ways. Without doubt, there are complexities when it comes to identity, situated understandings, and articulations of *who we are*.

In addition to "African American," the 1980s and 1990s witnessed the emergence of "Afro" identities throughout the African diaspora. Organizations of people of African descent in Brazil, Panama, Colombia, Venezuela, and Mexico, for example, often use "Afro" to define themselves. This does not mean that all people of African descent use "Afro" or "black" to define themselves, however. For that reason, it is also important to look at the intragroup naming processes and categories to see how people define themselves over time, how the state defines people, and how this is changing.

Overview of Book

This book is divided into four chapters. Chapter 1 is entitled "Stirring the *Sancocho*: Dominicanness, Race, and Mixture in Historical Context" and considers the history of immigration to the Dominican Republic with a focus on the state, the census, and categories of *mestizaje* (process of "race mixture"). Also, attention is paid to *blanqueamiento* (whitening) practices, the dictatorship of Rafael Leonidas Trujillo (1930–1961), and the construction of Dominican nationality, mixedness, and the institutionalization of the color category *indio* to represent the majority of Dominicans on the *cédula*, the national identification card.

Chapter 2, "*Indio*: A Question of Color," takes a close look at *indio* within its cultural context. This chapter details the process of obtaining a *cédula* (known as cedulazation) at the Junta Central Electoral (JCE) in Santiago. In

1998, *mulato* became a new color category on the new digitized *cédulas*—this was the first time that a mixed category implying African ancestry was used as an official state category on the *cédula*. This chapter explores the ways in which the JCE officials defined people in terms of color with *mulato* and *indio* being mixed categories.

Chapter 3, "The Dominican Diaspora: Blackening and Whitening and Mixture across Borders" explores the Dominican experience in the United States, where the Dominican racial system is called into question. Mixture is still preferred as a way of talking about Dominicans and race, but there has been a shift from *indio* to *mulato*, in part because of experience in the United States. Emerging from this experience is the idea of "here" (Dominican Republic) and "there" (United States) and the formation of a Dominican diaspora.

Chapter 4, "*Africanidad* and Afro-Dominican: Alliances, Organizations, and Networks in the African Diaspora," moves away from the idea of mixture and Dominicanness to the African diaspora and connections with other people and places throughout the Americas. The acclaimed Dominican poet Chiqui Vicioso talks about her experience in the United States, among African Americans, and her consciousness-raising process because of this experience. This chapter also focuses on a self-defined black feminist organization known as Casa de Identidad de las Mujeres Afro (House for the Identity of African-descended Women) founded in 1989 in Santo Domingo. For Identidad, "afro" becomes the umbrella term encompassing Afro-Dominican and *mulato/a* as a way of unburying the African past in reconstructing an identity that takes African ancestry into account.

The conclusion, "Unburying the African Past," recasts the idea of Dominican blackness as something that is consciously being unburied by Dominican scholars, intellectuals, and activists. While the introduction explores the concerted efforts by the state to bury blackness in history books and collective naming processes, the conclusion discusses how these efforts are being revisited and in many ways reversed. In the end, many Dominicans are reclaiming a sense of blackness—what it means to them locally, in the United States, and as part of the African diaspora—in an effort to unbury and make visible the African past and its legacy and impact on the present in terms of identity, circumstances, and experience.

Stirring the *Sancocho*

Dominicanness, Race, and Mixture in Historical Context

The history of *sancocho*, also Spanish for "pig slop," is all about raising the least
to the most, the ordinary to the extraordinary . . . Call us alchemists. The African Diaspora's always done what it could with what it's had, transmuting base
metals into gold. We've turned table scraps into feasts, curd into cheese, sour
grapes into wine, lemons into lemonade. It's hard work, disarming bombs.
And we season our efforts well. It's how Dominicans have alchemized into a
national dish the hodge-podge stew . . . Proudly we hold up humble bowls, as
an expression of identity, abundance, celebration, and communion.

  Nelly Rosario, "Feasting on *Sancocho* before Night Falls: A Meditation"

A bleaker, commonly held belief about *sancocho*'s origins points to the days of
slavery, during which there was surely little difference between the table scraps
thrown to the troughs and what was tossed aside to the slave quarters. Later,
sancocho came to refer to the "plantation stew" cobbled together by folks from
neighbors' crops . . . Today, *sancocho* has ascended as the revered national dish
of the Dominican Republic. It's served as tourist fare or on special occasions
or on Sundays or during inclement weather (Rosario 2007, 263–64).

Perhaps it is ironic that the origin of the national dish of the Dominican
Republic has its roots in slavery and an African past. Ironic because the discourse surrounding race and identity seldom references Africa—or being of
African descent—since Dominican racial identity, as constructed, privileges
mixture and emphasizes European and indigenous pasts. As a metaphor,
however, *sancocho* captures this sense of mixture as the national dish of the
Dominican Republic. As Rosario points out, *sancocho* is similar to a stew
filled with various ingredients—chicken, pork, and other meat, potatoes,
yucca, plantains, sweet potatoes, pumpkin, and corn on the cob in a flavorful
chicken stock—and a culinary favorite for family gatherings and celebrations. In no particular order, and not suggesting that all parts are equal,
these various ingredients represent diversity—ethnic, color, gender, class,
and regional—and the stock represents the common "stock" of Dominicanness or the sense of being Dominican in racial and national terms.

I remember the first time I had *sancocho*. It was in the fall of 1998, and my husband, David, our oldest daughter, Asha, and I were in the *campo* (countryside) in Dajabón near the Dominican-Haitian border with a friend we came to refer to as Tía (Aunt) Nancy and her family. It was prepared the traditional way in an outdoor kitchen in a large black pot over an open fire. Tía Nancy's niece started to stir the *sancocho*, but it didn't stir easily. The tubers and other ingredients created a resistance in the pot that was symbolic of the resistance of the enslaved people who had created the dish itself. After the *sancocho* simmered, we all sat down to enjoy a bowl.

Today, as the national dish, *sancocho* represents resultant mixture from generations of intermarriage and "marrying up" practices.[1] *Sancocho* is among other stews in the African diaspora that have been used to capture the sense of racial mixedness. For example, in the film *Black Is . . . Black Ain't* (1995), Marlon Riggs used gumbo to describe skin color variation and other differences among African Americans, while awara soup symbolized creolization in French Guyana in the film *Awara Soup* by Marie Clémence Blanc-Paes in 1995. The idea of *sancocho* is represented by the use of *indio* (a skin color category representing mixture) on the *cédula* (the national identification card) and *mestizo* on the census (in previous years).

In this chapter, using *sancocho* as a metaphor, I explore how racial and national identities were constructed and articulated in the Dominican Republic without a direct reference to an African past, both before and during the dictatorship of Rafael Leonidas Trujillo, hinting at the shift that has taken place in recent years to reclaim that past. This chapter gives a brief historical overview contextualizing Dominican racial socialization and illustrating how the African past was, in effect, buried as European immigrants entered the country and as Haitian and other Caribbean immigration to the Dominican Republic was curbed by immigration policies at the hand of Trujillo. Thus, this chapter seeks to make visible the ways in which Dominican blackness was constructed, buried, and relegated to being behind the ear (Candelario 2007).

Throughout the chapter, I describe the cultural significance of *dominicanidad* or Dominicanness with respect to *mestizaje* (process of "race mixture") and *hispanidad* (appreciation of everything Spanish). I suggest that Dominican peoplehood has encompassed, and continues to encompass, notions of race and that the nation was largely defined along racial lines as people moved back and forth across borders throughout the twentieth century. In the early 1900s, Dominicanness was defined vis-à-vis immigrant groups entering the county as well as Dominican nationals leaving the country, resulting in the stirring of the *sancocho*, moving away from ideas of an

African past, where the construction and articulation of Dominicanness was expressed in terms of being mixed, Catholic, and Spanish-speaking, moving away from the Africanity of *sancocho*.

"Somos una Mezcla" (We Are Mixed)

During interviews, whenever I asked a question about Dominican race and identity, the most common initial response was "Somos una mezcla. No somos puros" (We are mixed. We are not pure.) (Simmons 2005). The Dominican Republic is not unique in terms of espousing ideas of mixture. As in other places in Latin America and the Hispanic Caribbean, race and nation are connected in the formation of nationness (or sense of national belonging). In this case, *being Dominican* means *being mixed* where the idea of mixture is *a given* due to socialization, naming practices, and internalized notions of race. Historically, the Dominican state played an important role in the creation of racial, and later color, categories on the census and *cédula*, thereby naturalizing nationality in terms of an essential being. Dominicans interact with these categories on a daily basis, both formally (with institutions) and informally (with each other).

While mixture is a common feature throughout the African diaspora, it is the idea of mixture combined with specific categories that is perhaps unique to the Dominican case. In colonial and postcolonial contexts throughout the African diaspora, the term mulatto defined and categorized the offspring of Africans and Europeans (Yelvington 2001; Rahier 2003), but this is not how the Dominican state categorized Dominicans of similar ancestry. Mulatto implies having African ancestry, and this is not what the Dominican elite wanted to imply (Martínez-Vergne 2005). Instead, the preferred category was *indio* or *mestizo*, thus privileging Taíno (indigenous) and European ancestries (over African ancestry). As racial and color categories, *indio* and *mestizo* were created and re-created by the state and inhabited by people as they learned the cultural significance of the categories as a part of their own racialization (Omi and Winant 1994).

Indio was and continues to be the most prevalent color category used to talk about, identify, and define Dominican mixture. Some have argued that *indio* was a preferred state category since it did not signify Africanity (Torres-Saillant 2000; Howard 2001; Duany 2002) despite African presence on the island for much of the nineteenth century. *Indio* has a place on the national identification card while *mestizo* represented mixture on the Dominican census. *Mestizo* first emerged as a racial category on the census in

1935 and became a color category in 1950 (see appendix I). *Indio* became an official *cédula*[2] color category during the dictatorship of Trujillo although it was also used informally among Dominicans as an umbrella term encompassing a range of skin tones. The two most common color descriptors of *indio* are light (*claro*) and dark (*oscuro*), however, cinnamon (*canela*), medium light (*medio claro*), and medium dark (*medio oscuro*) are also used among other color terms.[3] On the *cédula*, however, the *indio* category represents the entire range of shades between *indio claro* and *indio oscuro*.

Again, the Dominican Republic is not alone in assigning racial or color categories based on ideas of mixture. Venezuela, Puerto Rico, and Brazil are among some of the other countries in the Americas that recognize skin color variation due to *mestizaje* or race mixture (Yelvington 2001; Whitten and Torres 1998; Wright 1990; Rahier 2003; Duany 2002; Twine 1998; Godreau 2002; Caldwell 2007). By way of comparison, the United States is not usually listed as a country with recognized ideas of mixture often because of the historic "one-drop rule" defining anyone with *any* African or black ancestry as black. However, before all people of African descent *became* black in the United States, some people were defined as mulattos. At that point in time, racial classifications tended to mirror those in Latin America and the Hispanic Caribbean with regard to African Americans (Simmons 2008). Before 1920, mulatto was a racial category on the U.S. census, and before that, there were categories such as octoroon and quadroon ("quantifying" the amount of "African" or black blood). These categories existed as a result of mixture stemming from the colonial period in the United States. In effect, over time, this mixture helped to create the range of skin tones we find in the black community today. In this way, African Americans and Dominicans are similar in terms of the range of skin color and also because of the intra-group color categories or what I term colorization practices. African Americans' color categories are very similar to that of Dominicans. Terms such as light-skinned, brown-skinned, and dark-skinned describe skin tone and color variation within the community and are commonly used among African Americans who are all defined in racial terms as black.

Looking at other examples in the Americas, we see similar patterns of color labeling and naming or colorization. In Venezuela,[4] socio-racial categories such as *pardo, casta, zambo, mulato, moreno,* and *negro* were used at different points in time to define, position, and quantify peoples of African descent (Wright 1990). Now, since official categories no longer exist, and the census no longer records or reports race, Venezuela claims to be a country without racial distinctions. Using "cafe con leche" (coffee with milk) as a way of talking about and describing mixture resulting from years of *blanquea-miento*, or whitening practices, Venezuelans, like Dominicans and African Americans, encouraged ideas of "marrying up" (marrying a person with a lighter skin tone) to "lighten" offspring and to "improve the race."

We tend to think of *blanqueamiento* in biological terms, but it was also a cultural strategy as Safa has noted (2005, 1998). In Puerto Rico, for example, this cultural strategy involved attaching negative values to blackness and positive values to whiteness that Puerto Ricans then internalized (Whitten and Torres 1998; Godreau 2002). Defined by hair texture as well as facial features and skin color, white, black, and mulatto represent three primary physical "types" in Puerto Rico (Duany 1998). It has also been argued that the racial/color spectrum is more fluid in Puerto Rico than in the United States and reflects more of a continuum, or "rainbow" (Rodriguez 2000).

In Venezuela, the state effectively reminded Afro-Venezuelans of their ancestry, their racial heritage, and their social location and place in society through cartoons and caricatures despite not having racial categories on the census (Wright 1990). This is the key difference between Venezuela, Puerto Rico, and the Dominican Republic. In the Dominican Republic, negative values and stereotypes were *not* linked to *mulato* or dark-skinned Dominicans—they were linked to Haitians. Dominicans were not reminded of their ancestral ties to slavery—they were reminded of Haitians' past with slavery (Moya Pons 1995). Moya Pons (1995) suggests that the agrarian, cattle-ranching society in the Dominican Republic after the Spanish Creoles emigrated to other countries, during the end of the nineteenth century and the beginning of the twentieth, was a significant shift that left much of the sugar production activities in Haiti—possibly contributing to the idea of slavery being associated with Haiti (Martínez 1999). Although this cattle-ranching period continued to witness social stratification, poor Spanish Creoles, mulattos, and blacks were considered to be more or less in the same economic situation and involved in trade with Haiti.

Race, Nation, and Social Class: The Simmering of the *Sancocho*

By the mid-1800s, the Dominican Republic and Haiti had become nation-states with an intertwined history and complex relationship. *El pueblo dominicano* (the Dominican people) emerged as a way of talking about Dominican culture, experience, and race (see Hoetink 1982). The *pueblo* evokes a sense of peoplehood and shared experience. It also tends to homogenize difference as people are linked to territories: "in linking territory with a sense of peoplehood, nationalist projects homogenize difference by defining shared characteristics which mark the persons who inhabit that territory as the same 'kind' of people" (Medina 1997, 760). When differences exist, they are actually homogenized in the formation of nationness and peoplehood, and this homogenization takes place in the form of historical memory and the creation of a "we" as products and achievements of history (Foster 1991). Importantly, homogenization only encompasses certain traits, histories, and "types" in the formation of peoplehood. With the increased movement of people across borders, the articulation of a homogenized "we" is in relation to a not-yet homogenized "they." As groups enter new territories, they often find themselves defined in different ways and as "friends" and "strangers" with attention given to their "place" of origin (Simmel 1950).

While individuals and groups are defined and labeled as friends and strangers, they are also subjected to other processes of inclusion and exclusion. In her work, Ong (1996) found that Asian immigrants were subjected to either a "whitening" (affluent Chinese immigrants) or "blackening" (Cambodian "refugees") process when entering the United States and were treated differently based on their human capital (that is, money and education) and social capital (that is, family and other networks). Haitian immigrants in the Dominican Republic are considered to have little human and social capital and are subjected to a blackening process while European immigrants are subjected to the whitening process because of their human and social capital.

For Afro–Latin American and Caribbean people, social class and race have been, and continue to be, interconnected. Looking historically, we have a better sense of prevailing perspectives and attitudes regarding race. By the time of the Atlantic slave trade and the formation of the New World, European colonizers already had firm ideas of who Africans were although they were not sure about Native Americans (Wade 1997). It has been well documented that Europeans considered Africans and Native Americans to be inferior, and for that reason, they were assigned a social status based on prejudicial beliefs (Baker 1998). The social status of Africans and Native Americans determined whether or not they were enslaved or indentured workers as well as the type of work they performed. Despite emancipation and "racial democracies" throughout the region, this previously imposed "inferior" status on both African- and indigenous-descended groups continues to have a lingering effect today—so much so that ideas of racial difference led to the formation of a stratified society in the United States (Baker 1998) and throughout the Americas. These differences link class and race in Latin

America today: "By the nineteenth century it had become well established that African origin implied slavery. The Cuban economy run with slave labour perpetuated colour prejudice as a conventional device to justify slavery. The criterion chosen to classify the population hierarchically was physical appearance and particularly skin colour, this initially being the most consistent and also the most salient difference between the two groups" (Martínez-Alier 1989, 80).

Throughout Latin America and the Caribbean, social class and status hierarchy were established along racial and color lines. Class is often evident when examining differences in Latin America, but what may be less evident is the racial foundation on which the class system is based. Torres (1998, 288) aptly put it: "In the past, scholars who compared the racial-color continuum in Latin America and the Spanish-speaking Caribbean to the racial bifurcation in the United States and elsewhere demonstrated how race and class are interrelated (Hoetink 1967; Mintz 1971; Duany 1985). However, for the most part, these scholars argued that class relations in Latin America and the Spanish-speaking Caribbean took precedence over race relations, and thereby they failed to analyze how discourses about class relations euphemize race and provide a means to deny the existence and persistence of racist practices." Social class is tied to ideas of race and rooted in the colonial period when people were assigned a class-based status due to their perceived racial difference. As we look throughout the Americas, we notice that Africans had the lowest status when compared to American Indians (Wade 1997), the Chinese (Martínez-Alier 1989), and East Indians (Segal 1993). And again, labor was assigned to individuals based on perceived racial "types." For example, in the Dominican Republic, cutting sugar cane has been historically linked to slavery and associated with "Haitians' work."

Historical Construction of Dominicanness

How do the ideas of belonging to a nation and changing notions of peoplehood take shape over time and space as people migrate? As people move across borders, they become involved in a process where racial and national identities are co-constructed in the articulation of nationness (Harrison 1995; Williams 1989). I had read about immigration to and from the Dominican Republic and wondered what this meant in terms of a Dominican national identity as well as race and color categories. I decided to take a historical approach to look at immigration by considering census data as well as documents discussing immigration strategies to see what this revealed about race and nation as well as changing notions of identity. Looking historically provides insight into some of the more salient periods when some identities were articulated over others in the construction of nationness. The historical data reveal that Dominicanness has its roots in periods of emigration out of and immigration into the Dominican Republic, where ideas of race and culture were constantly re-formed with distance from blackness.

I identified and named two historical periods in the Dominican Republic, 1900–1930 and 1930–1961, to show how early ideational seeds were planted that came to shape the present along the lines of racial and national identities. The first period I consider is the pre- Trujillo era (U.S. occupation era) when Dominicans were referred to in local print media as being "of color," and the second period is the dictatorship, known as the *trujillato*, where these ideas were challenged and changed; Dominicanness was firmly cemented during the *trujillato*.

The census and other historical data suggest that much of what happened in 1930–1961 was a reaction to earlier circumstances involving a decrease in the population of Spanish Creoles and an increase of *negro* immigrants (Moya Pons 1998). There was also a growing anti-Haitian sentiment during the *trujillato* that was rooted in what was called the "Haitian Invasion" of the Dominican Republic in 1822–1844 when the Spanish colony was unified as one with Haiti (Paulino 2005; Silié 1976; Derby 1994).[5]

During the unification, the Haitian president, Jean Pierre Boyer, invited different foreign groups to come and reside in what was then Haiti. One of these groups consisted of black Americans affiliated with the African Methodist Episcopal Church (AME) in Philadelphia (M. Davis 1994, 1983, 1981). They left the United States and settled in Samana Bay, on the eastern peninsular coast of the Dominican Republic (see Mayes forthcoming 2009 for a discussion of immigration and experience in San Pedro).

Today, some have maintained the tradition of speaking English and are still members of the AME Church. In addition to the black Americans, Jehovah's Witnesses also settled in the Dominican Republic during this time. These two groups alone introduced more religious diversity in a place where the Catholic Church had a very strong influence. Before the unification, the Catholic Church had been the "church" of the people. Along with increasing religious diversity, Boyer also ordered the abolition of slavery in the Dominican Republic. Some scholars refer to this period in history as Haitian "liberation" instead of Dominican "invasion" (Paulino 2005).

Gente de Color (People of Color)

> Historians have shown that the present-day population of the Dominican Re-
> public is the result of the intense mixture of peoples of European, African,
> and, to a lesser extent, Amerindian origin. By the end of the 18th century,
> the majority of Dominicans were classified as colored—that is mulattos and
> blacks or, in contemporary parlance, pardos and morenos.
>
> Jorge Duany, "Reconstructing Racial Identity"

I found it interesting that there were references to being "of color" in the early
1900s in Dominican newspapers. Widely used today to encompass African
Americans, Latinos/as, Asian, and Native Americans in the United States,
the term "colored" was used to describe the majority of the Dominican population during a time of increased immigration to the Dominican Republic
from Europe and other places. The majority of the "of color" population was
defined as "mestizo" according to the census at the end of the nineteenth
century and the beginning of the twentieth. In fact, in the first Dominican
national census of 1920, there were three official state-sanctioned racial categories (*blanco*, *mestizo*, and *negro*). The *mestizo* category included both the
"mixed" population as well as Asian immigrants, and *negro* included darker-
skinned Dominicans as well as Haitians (see appendix D). *Mestizo* came to
categorize the population in racial terms on the census, while the Dominican print media used "of color" to refer to the majority of Dominicans.

It is often the case that an elite group creates the official state categories.
And in the case of the Dominican Republic, the elite was composed of very
light-skinned people (Martínez-Vergne 2005; Mayes forthcoming 2009). In
fact, since the emigration of Spanish Creoles at the end of the nineteenth
century and the beginning of the twentieth, a light-skinned *mestizo/mulato*[6]
elite has been the normative group (Martínez-Vergne 2006; San Miguel
2006).[7] Torres-Saillant (2000, 134) elaborates: "The decay of the plantation
and the virtual destitution of whites helped to break down the social barriers
between the races, stimulating interracial marital relations and giving rise to
an ethnically hybrid population. The racial integration and ethnic hybridity
that characterized seventeenth-century Santo Domingo explain the emergence of the mulatto as the predominant type in the ethnic composition of
the Dominican population." The *mestizo/mulato* elite defined everyone in
relation to themselves; Haitians were *negro* (black), and the European immigrants were *blanco* (white). Locally, *mestizo* was the category of choice even
as scholars outside of the Dominican Republic often used *mulato* to define
and describe Dominicans.[8]

Dominican newspapers in the early twentieth century used terms like *de color* (of color) in advertisements and in opinion pieces. In *El Diario*, in one advertisement for a particular hair product, Dominicans were described as being "damas y caballeros de color" (ladies and gentlemen of color).[9] On the first page of *El Diario*, the Dominican Republic was listed as being in Santiago de los Caballeros, Dominican Republic and "in the West Indies."[10] This was 1918, and the fact that the Dominican Republic was imagined to be composed of people of color and "in the West Indies" during this time is very significant because it suggests a plantation past, slavery, and a connectedness with other Caribbean islands. This image soon changed during the dictatorship of Rafael Leonidas Trujillo (1930–1961) with references to "the West Indies" and anything black or African being buried in the historical memory.

Against the *de color* backdrop, there was immigration to the Dominican Republic (as throughout the Americas at the time). Tables A and C in the appendices show the type of immigration that occurred to the Dominican Republic at the beginning of the twentieth century. I wanted to have a sense of the type of immigration that was taking place, how the state documented this immigration, and what this immigration meant in terms of race and constructions of race over time. The Santiago census of 1903 was the first census to provide a way of categorizing race and national origin. We see that early on there was an emphasis on classifying people as "Dominican" and "non-Dominican, paying close attention to national origin and gender."[11] Of note in the 1903 census (see appendix A) is that there were more Dominican women than men; however, there were more Spanish, Italian, Arab (Lebanese), American, Cuban, and Haitian men than women. The prevalence of more men than women had implications for intermarriage with Dominican women. In fact, many of the upper-middle-class women I met in Santiago talked about having European and/or "Arab" heritage. In 2003, Reina, one of our neighbors, invited us over for a party. "Vamos a comer la comida árabe" (we're going to eat Arab [Lebanese] food). We had *quipe* (kibbe), tabouli, and other foods. Now *quipe* is part of the larger Dominican culture and cuisine where people go out and enjoy *quipe* as they would empanadas. At the time, of the nine families in our building, two families claimed Lebanese ancestry, one family claimed Mexican ancestry (and made Mexican food on special occasions), one family was from Guatemala, and the rest of the families described themselves as Dominican and did not refer to other ancestries.

While different nationalities were named in 1903 in the census, it wasn't until the 1916 census in Santiago (see appendix B) that the category of "foreign" emerged to categorize Dominican and non-Dominican, creating a "we—they" or "us—them" dichotomous relationship. "Dominican" and "Foreign" became categories signifying national belonging and "not belonging" and religion began to be represented by the categories of "Catholic" and "Other." "Catholic" later became understood as a part of the definition of *being* Dominican. As in 1903, there were more women than men, which could have led to intermarriage with Dominican men, over time contributing to the idea of the Dominican *sancocho*.

In 1916, resident foreigners were surveyed and categorized according to national groups (see appendix C). In total, there were seventeen national origins representing the 1,607 foreigners as a result of this wave of immigration to the Dominican Republic (and U.S. 1916–1924 occupation[12]). During this time, we see that there were more Haitians in Santiago (and in other places in the Dominican Republic) than there had been in 1903 because of a growing need for labor in the sugar cane fields for the export of sugar (Martínez 1999). The "Arabs" (Lebanese) were an active part of the commercial life as merchants, and the Chinese were involved in laundry services and restaurants (Hoetink 1982). All of this points to a growing diversity in the Dominican Republic.

The first national census of 1920 reveals some of the most important and defining markers in the Dominican Republic of the time, classifying Dominicans and foreigners with attention to religion and racial composition (see appendix D). There were three national racial categories in the Dominican Republic in 1920 (*blanco*, *mestizo*, and *negro*). *Blanco* included both European-descended Dominican nationals and foreigners of European descent. *Mestizo* referred to "mixed" Dominicans and also included Asians (this changed in later years), and *negro* referred to dark-skinned Dominicans and included Haitians. I suspect that *negro* also included the immigrants from other Caribbean countries who, along with Haitian laborers, also worked in the sugar cane fields. These immigrants were often from the British, Dutch, and Danish Islands of the Caribbean.[13]

It is important to note that the United States occupied both the Dominican Republic and Haiti during this time. While in the Dominican Republic, from 1916 to 1924, the U.S. Marines established a U.S. military government and the Guardia Nacional Dominicana (Dominican National Guard, or GND); this is where the "post-intervention" president Rafael L. Trujillo received his military training. When I examined some of the declassified memos from this time period, from the U.S. Department of State, it was clear that the United States viewed Haiti as a "black country." This was language that was used. What is less clear, however, is how the United States viewed the Dominican Republic in relation to Haiti. Around this same time in the United States, the mulatto category was dropped from the census, and all mulattos legally *became* black due to the historic "one-drop rule" defining anyone with any African "blood" as black (Davis 1991; Smedley 1993).

Since the idea of mulattos existed in the United States, would the U.S. Marines view *mulato* Dominicans as they did mulattos in the United States? Perhaps, but the United States had a different racial history with black and mulatto people, power relationships, eventual white-black relational categories, legal segregation, and institutional forms of racism restricting access to resources. But as the United States exercised military control of both Haiti and the Dominican Republic, the question remains: Did the Marines play a role in the distinction between *mulato* and *negro* as such a distinction existed in the United States? Even when mulattos became black in the United States they often enjoyed an elevated social status (Davis 1991). In fact, some mulattos were part of organizations and social group based on *being mulatto*—as was the case in Charleston, South Carolina and the founding of the Brown Fellowship Society.[14]

Immigration to the Dominican Republic during the early 1900s facilitated a process by which the nation-state began to define itself as Dominican, as mixed (*mestizo*), and as Catholic. While many Spanish Creoles emigrated from the Dominican Republic to other countries in the region, Haitians and black Caribbean people immigrated to the Dominican Republic to work in the sugar cane fields. The fact that there was a decrease in the Spanish Creole population (a *blanco* group) concurrent with an increase in Haitian and other Caribbean immigrants (*negro* groups) is very significant as the racial discourse soon moved away from one of color (*de color*) to one embracing everything Spanish (*hispanidad*).

Hispanidad: Rafael Leonidas Trujillo and the Distance from *Gente de Color* (1930–1961)

> The old aristocracy had marked their superiority through the metaphor of "blood," which indexed filiation with the respectable families of either the interior town of Santiago or Santo Domingo, the capital, while expressing at least an ideal type of phenotypical whiteness or "purity of blood." In this predominantly mulatto society, race and class were inextricably associated and mutually reinforcing. The closed character of the traditional elite can be seen in the proclivity of the old families for cousin marriage, which was the norm, particularly in the interior, into the 1930s.
>
> Lauren Derby, "The Dictator's Seduction"

The period before Trujillo witnessed emigration from and immigration to the Dominican Republic. All of these groups now residing in the Dominican Republic were listed and recorded on the national census as part of the national body. Haitians did not seem to have any more prominence than any other national group. All of this changed as Rafael Trujillo came to power and institutionalized categories and immigration policies that would later have an effect on how the Dominican nation would be reimagined and reconfigured at the end of the twentieth century.

During the *trujillato*, the racial discourse shifted from being *de color* to *hispanidad* where everything "Spanish" was embraced (Sagás 2000; Betances 1995; Cassá 1975; Winn 1992). This meant identifying with and appreciating Spanish culture and society. In this way, Spain became a point of reference and a link to understanding Dominican life and people. The idea of mixture still existed as it did before, but Trujillo gave social currency to the term *indio* as representing Dominican mixture. So, on the one hand, there was a privileging of Spanish ancestry while, on the other hand, there was a simultaneous recognition of mixture highlighting Spanish-indigenous ancestry. While *indio* literally means "Indian," or "indigenous," it socially represents skin color variation due to mixture over time. It is most often used as a color category, but it also serves as a racial "type" on the national identification card (see chapter 2) since it defines a racial location between black and white. *Mestizo*, however, did not disappear; it continued to be used as a racial category on the census during this same time. For light-skinned Dominican elites, *mestizo* and *indio* were preferred race/color categories over *mulato* since they did not imply African ancestry. For that reason, a *mulato* identity was not articulated on a national level—*mestizo* was used in place of *mulato* on the census, and *indio* became the institutionalized color category on the *cédula*.[15]

One of the first steps Trujillo made in casting the international image of the Dominican Republic was by hosting international fairs (Derby 2000) and displaying photos of Spanish immigrants and very light-skinned women (with captions stressing the beauty of Dominican women).[16] Perhaps it was an attempt to change the image of the Dominican Republic from being constructed as a country of people of color to a very light, almost white ideal. A cursory glance at descriptions of the Dominican Republic from the 1930s to the 1960s, from outside the country, often used words like "mixed" or "mulatto" to describe the majority of the population. Trujillo went against this and promoted *mestizo* and *indio* to racially represent the majority of Dominicans instead of *mulato*.

The shift away from being "de color" not only pertained to race, color, and ancestry, but also to geography. Dominican newspapers, like *El Diario*, that had once referred to the Dominican Republic as being in the West Indies dropped the reference all together. I suggest this was because of emergent ideas of *hispanidad*, which called for references to Spain, not to the Afro-Caribbean region. During the *trujillato*, the term "people of color" became a way of talking about Haitians who were blamed for the "browning" of the Dominican Republic during the unification of the island in 1822–1844. The idea was that Haiti was Africa, and Africa was Haiti; Haitians became the "undesired" immigrants[17] while Europeans became the "desired" immigrants. Looking toward Europe, Trujillo issued a "call for immigrants" in the newspapers and government memos (see appendices E and F); this was the beginning of a targeted immigration policy to promote *blanqueamiento* (whitening) in the Dominican Republic. People from Europe also immigrated to other Latin American countries and also to the United States (Roediger 2006; Foner 2002) during the early twentieth century. While Europeans did settle in the Dominican Republic, more went to other countries in the region, such as Argentina. So, Trujillo was not as successful in attracting the number of Europeans as other countries. Nonetheless, Trujillo encouraged European immigration while restricting the immigration of Dominicans to other countries (Torres-Saillant and Hernández 1998).

While the Dominican Republic grew in diversity, the census also shows that ideas of Dominicanness were forming in terms of categorizing who was *Dominican* and who was *foreign*. Returning to the idea of the *sancocho* for a moment, immigration played a role in facilitating a process of diversity, but at the same time, there were homogenizing efforts to define what being Dominican was and what it meant. The National Population Census of May 13, 1935 (see appendix G) reflected this shift. Like previous censuses, this one made distinctions between Dominicans and foreigners, however, for the first time, foreigners of "all races" was a category, perhaps also because the Dominican Republic was now being seen and reinforcing itself as an independent state, and Haitians were counted and categorized in terms of gender and location (urban/rural zones). This isolation of Haitians is significant because their presence was recorded two years before the *matanza*, or massacre, of the Haitians at the request of Trujillo (Turits 2002; Derby and Turits 1993; Paulino 2005).

While Dominicanness and ideas of race and nation were firmly planted during the *trujillato*, social class and status also took shape. Someone commented to me during an interview that "even the poorest Dominican is better off than a Haitian," referring to the poverty and the conditions in which many Haitians find themselves. Haitians residing in the Dominican Republic are often marked as "poor," "dirty," "disease-ridden," and people who are to be "feared" (because of Haitian voodoo and the "belief" that "Haitians eat people").[18] Strong anti-Haitian nationalist sentiments emerged that led to the mistreatment and discrimination of Haitians over time (Sagás 2000; Silié 1976; Paulino 2005; Adams 2006; Dore Cabral 1987).[19] As Derby (1994, 495) suggests, anti-Haitianism has a long history in the Dominican Republic: "Anti-Haitianism must be understood as more than racism as such. It arose initially as consciousness of colonial difference, an identity marked first by language (French versus Spanish; the import of the linguistic ascription of alterity still lingers today), then by a series of derivative collective assertions of differences originating in colonial rivalries between the French and Spanish. Anti-Haitianism's second layer of meaning stemmed from Saint Domingue's (which later became Haiti) former economic supremacy and colonial grandeur, in stark contrast to the poverty of the Spanish colony."

While *hispanidad* advanced the absolute appreciation of everything "Spanish," it also firmly established and rooted the idea of *blanqueamiento*, and by extension, *mestizaje*. It was said that Trujillo declared that the Dominican Republic was the most Spanish of the Americas and that Dominicans should identify with everything Spanish (Moya Pons 1998; Winn 1992). Toward this end, he ordered the rewriting of Dominican history textbooks in order to erase the presence of West Africans and to suggest that the Africans who were brought as slaves to the Dominican Republic were from North Africa (Winn 1992; Torres-Saillant 1995). This burial of the African past extended to music and the national music of the Dominican Republic, the merengue, as Trujillo ordered the removal of one of the drums used in merengue music because it sounded "too African" (Austerlitz 1997). The *sancocho*, once prepared and consumed by slaves—at once recognizing their resourcefulness and resistance—came to represent immigration and then the homogenizing effect of mixture as in *mestizo* and *indio*. *Sancocho* was out of context and recast in the national imaginary. The newly altered historical accounts became part of the official Dominican history as it was told and retold in textbooks as well as in oral tradition, explaining, in part, why many Dominicans do not consider themselves to be of African descent—they did not *learn* that they were of African descent in terms of their socialization (Simmons 2006). The category *indio* was attractive to Trujillo—it implied racial mixture and could be used as a color denominator to describe skin color (for example, *indio claro*/light-skinned or *indio oscuro*/dark-skinned) without referencing African ancestry. While *indio* never appeared on the census, Trujillo was effective in institutionalizing it as he set in motion its usage on the *cédula*, the national identification card (Torres-Saillant 1995).

The construction of *indio* as a non-black, mixed, race/color category is in relation to Haitians, who were defined on the census as black.[20] Again, as Moya Pons (1998) suggests, Haitians were closely associated with slavery, strenuous manual labor, and *being* black. Over time, the usage of *indio* color descriptors and categories had the effect of distancing Dominicans from their African heritage and ideas of blackness in an attempt to create an affinity toward Spanish ideals against an indigenous (Taíno) landscape. The effort to advance *hispanidad* not only meant a cultural affiliation with Spain but also a phenotypic one. *Blanco* was used to classify someone of Spanish (or other European) ancestry, and *negro* was used to classify someone of African ancestry (Haitian or other West Indian).

Trujillo was successful in creating images, giving meaning to categories, and maintaining a level of appreciation of everything Spanish and scorning anything that had to do with Haiti. Looking at some of his memos and other correspondence, in Bernardo Vega's work (1986), it is clear that Trujillo created a systematic fear of Haitians and a belief that they were not to be trusted and needed to be closely monitored. He did this by reminding people that the Dominican Republic had been "invaded" by Haiti in 1822 and that this was never to happen again. In interview after interview, people commented on how Haitians had invaded the Dominican Republic and symbolically darkened the country.

Relying on the media and the educational system to perpetuate these ideas, Trujillo in effect not only orchestrated a racialized immigration project but also planted and sowed seeds for growing anti-Haitian sentiment that culminated in the extermination of thousands of Haitians residing in the Dominican Republic in 1937, an event known as the *matanza* (massacre).

> The Haitians living near the border were completely marginal to Dominican society and the territory they occupied functioned as an extension of Haiti. Haitian currency circulated freely in the Cibao, the main agricultural region of the country, and in the south it circulated as far as Azua, only 120 kilometers from Santo Domingo. Trujillo did not want to accept that fact. He traveled to the frontier at the beginning of October 1937, and there gave a speech announcing that the occupation by Haitians of the frontier territories must not continue. Afterwards, he ordered that all Haitians remaining in the country be exterminated. In the days following October 4, 1937, the army assassinated all Haitians on sight. Eighteen thousand Haitians were killed. The only ones able to save their lives were those who managed to cross

the border and those protected by the sugar mills, which did not want to lose their Haitian labor force. (Moya Pons 1995, 368)

Trujillo promoted mixture and "needed" European immigrants to help "lighten" certain areas of the country. Toward that aim, Trujillo granted permission for Jewish refugees to settle in the northern part of the Dominican Republic (see appendix H) at the request of his daughter who had befriended a Jewish woman in Europe years earlier. The irony here though is that the Jewish refugees, once viewed as "non-white" in Nazi Germany, represented whiteness to Trujillo, and that the Dominican Republic was a refuge for the Jews and a place of peril for many Haitians. Trujillo's acceptance of the refugees also gave him a way to redeem himself in the eyes of the international community after word had spread about the *mantanza.*

Following international and public protest against this horrific massacre,[21] Trujillo allegedly paid large sums of money to Haiti for damages and suggested that there had been border disputes between the two neighboring countries. The present-day tensions between Dominicans and Haitians, as well as contemporary images, have their roots in the *trujillato.* Importantly, despite efforts to remove Haitian immigrants, they and their descendants still have a presence in the Dominican Republic. Although their lives in the Dominican Republic are difficult, involving performing arduous tasks, working long hours for little pay (for example, in construction work, sugar cane fields, and other plantations, and so forth), and in the face of tremendous discrimination, many Haitians continue to cross the border in search of employment opportunities.

The effect of both the *matanza* on the *negro* population and the immigration of Europeans on the *blanco* population is evident when comparing the census data of 1935 to that of 1950 (see appendix I). There was a significant increase of *blancos* between 1935 and 1950, and at the same time, a decrease in *negros* (following the *matanza* of the Haitians in the Dominican-Haitian border communities). There was also an increase in *mestizos* and *amarillos* during this same time. Trujillo's targeted immigration policies were at play, and while the idea was to increase the mixed population, the group that increased the most was *blanco.* Some of the newly arrived Europeans intermarried with Dominicans, but others did not. In fact, there were communities of Spanish and Italian immigrants who formed their own enclaves and social groups. The Spanish established a Spanish society in 1965 and the exclusive country club Centro Español (Spanish Club) in 1966. Today, the Centro Español is still the most exclusive country club in Santiago with an initial membership fee of more than nine thousand U.S. dollars, making it "the club" of upper-middle-class and wealthy Dominicans. According to its website (centroespanol.com), the Centro Español "surge por la necesidad que tenia la pequeña colonia española" (came about because of the needs of the small Spanish colony). Today, according to the website, the Centro Español is "un club social y deportivo creado y dedicado fundamentalmente al fomento de las culturas Española y Dominicana" (a social and sports club dedicated fundamentally to the growth of the Spanish and Dominican cultures). It was my experience that people with Spanish ancestry said that they were Dominican but also referred to having Spanish heritage. It was also the case that Dominicans who claimed Spanish, Lebanese, Argentine, and/or Italian ancestry were the ones who were classified as white on their *cédulas* if they were very light-skinned with straight hair (distinguishable physical features that marked them as white).

There are some significant shifts that followed the census of 1935 that set a precedent. In particular, the census of 1950 moved away from race and racial classifications in favor of color, and for the first time color and nationality were defined in the following terms:[22]

Color—Se determinó el color, no la raza, de las personas empadronadas. Se clasificó la población en blanca, negra, mestiza y amarilla, según el caso, y de acuerdo a la apreciación del empadronador, quien fué instruído para que salvo en circunstancias especiales, hiciese esta pregunta (xiv).

Nacionalidad—Esta pregunta cubrió dos aspectos: en primer lugar se anotó: "dominicano," "naturalizado dominicano," o "extranjero," de acuerdo con la declaración de la persona interrogada. Si ésta declaraba ser naturalizada dominicana, en un segundo renglón, como consecuencia a esta primera anotación, se hizo constar a que nacionalidad pertenecía antes de haber adquirido la nacionalidad dominicana. Si por el contrario la persona declaró ser extranjera, en este mismo segundo renglón se anotaba su nacionalidad (xiv).

(Color—The color, not the race, was determined of registered people. The population was classified into white, black, mixed, and yellow/Asian [Chinese] categories, according to each case, and according to the census taker, who was instructed to ask questions [about the person's color] in special circumstances [when color could not be determined].

Nationality—This question covered two aspects: first the census taker noted: "from the Dominican Republic," "naturalized in the Dominican Republic," or "foreigner," depending on the person's declaration of nationality. If naturalized in the Dominican Republic, on a second line, as a result, it was noted that there was a different nationality before having acquired Dominican nationality. However, if the person declared to be foreign, on this same second line, the nationality was noted.)

This shift may have followed other trends in the region moving toward the idea of a racial democracy with no "distinct" racial groups (like in Brazil and Venezuela). By definition, *mestizaje* involves racial mixture, and if *mestizaje* and *blanqueamiento* were the objectives during the *trujillato*, the ideal would be a mixed one with a range of color possibilities, not racial ones. In 1950, we also see a wedding of color and nation in the categorization of "La República," (the republic); this was used on the census for the first time in 1950 (see appendix J) as a complete representation of the population. The year 1950 also witnessed an increase in religious categories (see appendix K); Buddhist and Adventist were among the new categories added to the census of 1950. The Dominicanization process would soon emphasize Roman Catholicism and the Spanish language.

The perceived social and cultural threats against Dominican people in terms of language, religion, and cultural practices were clearly a part of feared Haitianization of the Dominican Republic. Dominicanization countered Haitianization by solidifying ideas of "who Dominicans were" in terms of mixture, language, religion, and *hispanidad*. In other words, "We are not like *them*."

In theory and practice, the Dominicanization process sought to define the nation in terms of its members, affirm the importance of religion (Roman Catholicism), and assert the importance of language (Spanish). During the Trujillo period the government monitored the usage of Kreyol in part through censuses and took preliminary efforts to prevent this language from being spoken (see appendix L). On the one hand, Kreyol was described by officials as a strange language, and on the other hand, as a dialect with a direct comparison to Spanish as the "superior" language, and the preferred one. It was believed that Spanish needed to be introduced as a way to increase the sense of patriotism in the Dominican Republic. Yet, in order to implement programs to dissuade some religious practices and languages, the state had to first identify them, and the census helped to facilitate this process.

The *sancocho*, arguably African in origin, has been recast as the national dish representing diversity and mixture without reference to African ancestry. The census data and memos point to the emergence of Dominicanness

and mixture cast as *mestizo*. The next chapter explores the institutionalization of another color category—*indio*—as a way to describe mixture and the
range of light to dark by the state (on the national identification card known
as the *cédula*), by people themselves as a form of colorization practice, and
in popular culture.

Indio

A Question of Color

Color and the New *Cédula*

Ethnically, the aboriginal population represented a category typified by non-whiteness as well as non-blackness, which could easily accommodate the racial in-betweenness of the Dominican mulatto. Thus, the regime gave currency to the term *indio* (Indian) to denominate the complexion of people of mixed ancestry. The term assumed official status in so far as the national identification card (*cédula*) gave it as a skin color designation during the three decades of the dictatorship and beyond. While in the minds of most Dominicans who use it the term merely describes a color gradation somewhere between the polar extremes of whiteness and blackness—in much the same way that the term mulatto does—the cultural commissars of the Trujillo regime preferred it primarily because the term was devoid of any semantic allusion to African heritage and would, thus, accord with their negrophobic definition of Dominicanness.

Silvio Torres-Saillant, "The Tribulation of Blackness"

... Cuando hablamos del dominicano hoy día, étnicamente no somos taínos, españoles o africanos, ni siquiera la suma de los tres, sino una cosa diferente. Somos esencialmente mulatos, un resultado del blanco con el negro (... When we speak of the Dominican today, ethnically we are not Taínos, Spanish, or African, not even a sum of the three, but rather something different. We are essentially mulattos, a result of black and white).

Dagoberto Tejada Ortiz, *Cultura Popular e Identidad Nacional*

Ever since I first began research in the Dominican Republic in 1993, I wanted to observe the process of obtaining a *cédula* as a way of understanding how color is determined by the state. The *cédula* serves a dual purpose in that it is both a voter identification card and a primary identification that is used to open credit accounts, apply for loans, and establish utility services. In 1998, announcements were made in print and television media that new digitalized *cédulas* would be issued with a fingerprint along with a photograph and would replace all previously issued *cédulas*; everyone had to obtain the new one. Finally I had the opportunity to observe *cédulas* issued over the course of three weeks at the Junta Central Electoral (JCE) in Santiago.[1]

I wanted to learn if *indio*, as a category, was simply descriptive, or if it served more as a racial category or both. I was particularly interested in seeing how representatives of the state entered into negotiation with people about their color, if at all. I was fortunate to observe this process as well as interview several staff members about how they classify people. In doing so, I found that *indio* was becoming increasingly problematic for the staff members and among Dominicans in general.

Before observing the process, I first had to go through a series of introductions to people who were made aware of my research and intentions. This was done through a chain of social networks over the course of two weeks; a close friend introduced me to his cousin, who was the president of the JCE in Santiago, who then introduced me to the secretary, who in turn introduced me to one of his staff members, a woman named Celia who would be issuing the new *cédulas*. Celia took me around the building to make sure that I met everyone else and to let them know that I would be observing the process. Finally, after a meeting with the secretary and Celia, I would be allowed to shadow Celia and observe the issuance of *cédulas*.

The process was intended to update *cédulas* and to create a computer database for all *cédulas* to prevent election fraud. There was a buzz throughout the country as announcements were made about the new *cédulas* in local newspapers and on television. The focus was on whether or not *indio* was an appropriate category to represent color or if it was time to replace it with another category. The consensus in the media was that *indio* should be removed from the *cédula*, but there was disagreement about which category to use in its place. Two camps emerged; one promoting *mestizo* and the other promoting *mulato*. It was a fascinating time because of all of the attention given to the possibility of recasting Dominican mixed identity.

On July 13, 1998, the president of the Partido de la Identidad Dominicana (PID, Dominican Identity Party) was interviewed for an article entitled "El PID llama a sustituir el término 'indio' de la cédula" (PID calls for a substitution of *indio* on the *cédula*):

El presidente del Partido de la Identidad Dominicana, Aulio Collado Anico, sugirió una legislación para que cambie el calificativo de "indio" que se establece como color de la piel de la gran mayoría de los dominicanos en la cédula de identidad. El dirigente político considera incorrecta esa denominación, ya que obedece a prejuicios raciales históricos, cuando en realidad el color de la gran mayoría de los dominicanos no es blanco, negro, ni tampoco indio, sino que la mejor representación es el mestizo. Collado sugiere a la Junta Central Electoral que se propone a promover reformas legales, incluyendo la confección de una nueva cédula de identidad personal, para que trate de corregir esa deformación racial en pos de que el calificativo de indio sea sustituido. ("El Cibao" section of *Listin Diario* by Ricardo Santana, p. 1)

(The president of the Dominican Identity Party, Aulio Collado Anico, suggested a legislation that changes the "indio" designation of skin color that describes majority of Dominicans on the *cédula* of identification. The political leader considers this denomination to be incorrect, referring to historical racial prejudices, when in reality the color of the majority of Dominicans is not white, black, or *indio*; the best representation is *mestizo*. Collado suggests to the Junta Central Electoral that he intends to promote legal reforms, including the making of a new *cédula* of identification, to try and correct the racial deformation after *indio* is substituted.)

Pointing to historical racial prejudices, Anico recommended *mestizo*, not *mulato*, as a category that best represents the majority of Dominicans, whom he defined as not *blanco*, *negro*, or *indio*. Despite the PID's efforts and discussion in the media, *mestizo* was not introduced as a new category and did not in fact replace *indio*. However, Anico did raise an important issue that was debated in both print and television media—the issue of *indio* being an historically "incorrect" category.

I had the opportunity to speak at length with Celia as the state prepared to reissue a record number of *cédulas*.[2] We talked about the *indio* category, the PID's efforts to replace *indio* with *mestizo*, and the questioning surrounding *indio* as a category. Celia commented that she and other officials of the Junta Central Electoral had been told that *indio* would *not* be on the *cédula* and that it would be replaced with *mestizo* and that *mulato* would also be an official category. On the one hand, *mestizo* is a return to the past in terms of how being mixed was defined on the census, but on the other hand, the introduction of *mulato* was revolutionary because this was the first time that a state-sanctioned category suggesting African ancestry would be used to classify Dominicans in the twentieth century.

The following excerpts are from an interview that I conducted with Celia before the new *cédulas* were issued:

KIM: Can we talk about the changes in the *cédula*? You told me before

that *indio* was not going to be on the *cédula* this time. This is the first
time that it won't be on the *cédula*.

CELIA: Right. We used *indio* before. *Indio* does not exist.

KIM: What happened to suggest that *indio* does not exist?

CELIA: I don't know. I have the idea that *indio* means "indigenous," and
I realized that we are not indigenous—pure indigenous. We are mixed,
but there are no Indians here.

Here, Celia discusses the difference between *indio* as a color category (which
uses Taíno Indians as an historical referent) and as an indicator of indig-
enousness (indigenous being a term often used to define Amerindians and
Native Americans). *Indio* is often translated in English to mean "Indian"
when scholars write about and discuss cultural identity, but this is not the
connotative meaning of *indio*.[3] I asked this question during interviews to
have a better sense of what *indio* means to people culturally. I asked the
following questions among others: 1) What does *indio* mean (open-ended
question)?; 2) Are all Dominicans *indio* (yes/no)?; 3) Are Dominicans in the
United States *indio* (yes/no)?; 4) Does *indio* mean "Dominican," skin color,
indigenous, race (all yes/no responses).

Some of the responses to the question about the meaning of *indio* were:
"it is a type of color," "someone whose skin is darker than *blanca* but lighter
than *morena*," "someone whose skin color is not light (*claro*) or dark (*oscuro*)
but mixed," "light *moreno*," "a person who is not *blanca* or *negra*," "*trigueño*
color," "color that is not *blanco* or *negro* but a mixture of both," and "a mixture of *blanco* with *negro*." There were also responses directly linked to the
Taíno past, such as "a person with an indigenous culture," "a distinct race
and old culture," and "indigenous person." The majority of the responses to
this question, however, tended to reflect a sense of racial and/or color in-
betweenness. There was consensus that *indio* does not mean Dominican but
rather skin color and/or race.

It is an important distinction because Dominicans don't see themselves as
"Indian" but rather use a category linked to the Taíno past to define mixture.
The Taínos were believed to have a range of skin tones—from light to dark—
and *indio* captures the sense of in-betweenness and color without reference
to African ancestry.

I asked Celia about the color categories on the *cédula*:

KIM: For the cedulazation, what are the color categories? *Amarillo* . . .

CELIA: *Amarillo, mulato, blanco, negro,* and *mestizo.*

KIM: Do you think that *mestizo* is a substitute for *indio*?

CELIA: It comes from *indio* and is a way of talking about a mixture of *blanco* and *negro* like *mulato*—we don't think of ourselves as *mulatos* here. *Indio* used to refer to the Taínos—they called them *indios*.

Here, Celia also linked *mestizo* and *indio* by saying that *mestizo* "comes from *indio*," and in this way, *indio* is used to refer to the past and to the Taíno Indians and mixture. Importantly, she said that Dominicans do not think of themselves as *mulatos*. Dominicans did not think of themselves as being mulatto because this was not part of their racial enculturation. Instead, they learned that they were *mestizo* perhaps, but more appropriately *indio*. While this is changing now, in the past school textbooks tended to reinforce the idea of an *indio* identity as students learned about the Taíno and Spanish past without much information about the African presence on the island.

So, what was the difference between *mulato* and *mestizo* as categories?

KIM: Do you think there is a difference between *mulato* and *mestizo*? What is the difference?

CELIA: For us, *mulatos* are darker than *mestizos*, and *negros* are darker than *mulatos*.

KIM: And *amarillo*?

CELIA: *Oriental* [Asian].

KIM: And *blanco*?

CELIA: Europe . . . Germany . . .

KIM: The other day, someone said that *mestizo* refers to a mixture between Dominican and Haitian . . .

CELIA: No. Here, the mixture of Dominican and Haitian is *mulato* or *negro* because they are very dark, although there are Haitians of French ancestry [white]. Many of them are descendants of enslaved Africans. But a mixture of Dominican and Haitian is *mulato* because we are "a little bit" lighter than they are.

So, according to Celia, in terms of skin color gradation, *mestizo* is considered to be lighter than *mulato*, which is lighter than *negro*. Much of what Celia described comes from her own life experience, knowledge, and understanding of Dominicans' intra-group naming practices or colorization. Like other JCE officials, she was trained and had some consensus about the categories, what they meant, and how people should be defined according to color. Celia's comment that *mestizo* was not the appropriate category resulting from Dominican and Haitian mixture is important here because implicit in this account is that Haitians are darker than Dominicans and it is the dark skin that necessarily leads to *mulato* as a mixed category instead of *mestizo*. Her definition of *mestizo* is different from the one offered by the PID in its call to replace *indio* with *mestizo*. Celia also expressed what I found to be a prevalent sentiment in that even though there are *mulatos* in Haiti, Dominicans tend to think of Haitians as being *negro* and dark. A large part of the socialization has been to construct Dominicanness in relation to Haitianness, and this is often constructed in terms of black meaning Haitian and mixed meaning Dominican despite mixture in Haitians and dark skin among Dominicans. I witnessed two different exchanges where a person's Haitianness was called into question by Dominicans because of his or her light skin tone.

I was invited to have lunch with Luis and his family. Luis's father was a prominent doctor in Santiago, and his mother, as mentioned in the introduction, was a self-defined feminist and journalist in the city. His father had dark brown skin, and his mother white (she was born in Argentina and reared in Spain). Luis's parents described him and his siblings, as well as me, as being *mulato*. When I arrived for lunch, three of Luis's friends were there as well—two were Dominican and one was Haitian. The friend from Haiti was light in complexion, and she told me that Dominicans think of her as Dominican—never as Haitian—because of her skin tone. Another incident took place in our building with the building attendant, Michel. Michel was a dark-skinned man from Haiti who would return to Haiti every six months to one year to renew his work visa to work in the Dominican Republic. At the end of the semester, Renee, a CIEE student, came by our apartment with a friend from Haiti, Jean Pierre. A student at the PUCMM, Jean Pierre was very light in complexion and was always thought to be Dominican (by Dominicans and Haitians alike). When Renee introduced me to Jean Pierre, Michel was nearby and also greeted him. Michel greeted Jean Pierre in Spanish, while Jean Pierre continued to greet and speak to Michel in Haitian Kreyol. Michel continued in Spanish until Jean Pierre said, "Michel, I am speaking to you in Kreyol. I am Haitian." With a smile, Michel shook Jean Pierre's hand and said to him in Kreyol, "I thought you were Dominican." The conversation continued in Kreyol. These two examples show that phenotypic "signs of mixture" mark people as being Dominican.

Returning to the cultural significance of *mestizo*, I asked Celia about *mestizo* being a known category in Mexico as well as *indio* and about the institutionalization of *mestizo* on the *cédula* during the Trujillo regime:

KIM: Do you think that the category *mestizo* is used because of influence from Mexico?
CELIA: Could be. Because Mexicans have a similar color—not real dark, but not too light either.

KIM: I read that Rafael Trujillo institutionalized *indio* by placing it on the *cédula*.
CELIA: Yes. He established everything. He established *indio*—because he was racist. They [*trujillistas*] were racist. They said *indio* to avoid saying *negro*.

Here, Celia makes the connection between Trujillo and establishing *indio* as a category on the *cédula* as a conscious decision to move away from *negro*. Already a popular way of talking about and labeling color among Dominicans, *indio* was introduced on the *cédula* during the *trujillato* and became the only state-sanctioned category representing mixture until *mulato* was introduced in 1998 when Leonel Fernández was serving his first term as president of the Dominican Republic.

At this point when Celia and I were discussing the implications of removing *indio* as a category, all of the JCE staff members were under the impression that *mestizo* was going to replace *indio* on the *cédula*. I wanted to know how Celia thought people would react to being defined, all of a sudden, as *mestizo*:

KIM: What will happen during the cedulazation when a person who is used to being classified as *indio* will not be classified in that way since *indio* will not be on the *cédula* this time? What do you think the reaction will be?
CELIA: You don't have to ask them what color they are. You have the option to look at them and choose a color. For the most part, they accept what you choose. There are many people with different backgrounds, classes, and they know that you are working, and they accept what you choose.

Here, Celia makes the point that people are defined by state officials; they do not define themselves or check a box, for example. In fact, Dominicans have had few, if any, chances to define themselves officially. From the census to the *cédula*, state officials have assigned racial and/or color categories, and for the most part there has been no dispute over color, although I did witness a couple of situations where color was called into question when there was disagreement over which category to use. I return to this later in the chapter.

I met several Dominicans who were residents of the United States and who had returned to the Dominican Republic to visit family. They were planning on obtaining the *cédula* while they were in the country. I was interested to know if Dominicans in the United States played a role in the reconstruction of racial/color categories in the Dominican Republic as well as what their experiences with race in the United States were. I asked Celia about it:

KIM: Do you think that the experiences that Dominicans have in the United States have an influence here in terms of the categories like *indio*?

CELIA: I don't know. There are *indios* there, real *indios* [Indians]. There is the category *indio* there [in the United States] because there are pure Indians [in the United States]. In Mexico, there are pure Indians, and in many countries in Latin America, there are pure Indians. But here, no.

KIM: Have your relatives talked about their experiences in the United States with respect to racial classifications?

CELIA: Yes. I have a cousin in the United States, and she told me that the United States is racist . . . when one wants to rent an apartment. There is racism against Latinos. They cast aside (*sacar*) Latinos. The United States is, to us, a country that is very developed. Racism still exists there and here.

Here, Celia conflated *indio* (the color) with *indio* (Indian/Native American). Aware that there are Native Americans in the United States, Mexico, and in other countries, she intimated the difference in the Dominican usage of the term. It is important to distinguish how *indio* is understood and used in everyday discourse in the Dominican Republic. Dominicans do not consider themselves to be nor define themselves as "Indians." There's a difference between saying "un indio" (an Indian) and "indio claro," for example, which means light-skinned.

Celia commented that it was surprising to learn about racism in the United States because, to her, the United States is a developed country with opportunities for immigrants as well as American citizens. I followed this idea about racism in the Dominican Republic:

KIM: How is racism manifested here?

CELIA: Against the Haitians because of their color. We reject (*rechazar*) them. We don't cast them aside (*sacar*), but we reject them because of their color—they are dark—even though many of us have the same color.

KIM: Is there tension between light-skinned Dominicans and dark-skinned Dominicans?

CELIA: Yes. Sometimes. Although there are more light-skinned men (*claro*) with *india* women and more light-skinned women (*clara*) with dark-skinned men (*oscuro*). The color of one's skin does not change. We are human beings.

Celia suggested that Latinos/as in the United States are cast aside and suggested that this does not happen to Haitians in the Dominican Republic. She made the distinction between "rejecting" Haitians and "casting them aside." However, based on conversations with Haitians residing in the Dominican Republic, I'm not sure if they would agree. Many feel tremendous discrimination and rejection as raids continue to take place in the *bateys* (residential work communities), as citizenship is called into question, and as they are paid low wages for work. This same type of discrimination played out with dark-complexioned African Americans on the CIEE exchange program I directed when they were confronted by Dominican police, thought to be Haitian, asked to pay more for food and drinks, and denied entry into some establishments (Simmons 2008).

I asked Celia about Haitians' color classification, and she said that they would most often be *negro*. As we talked about the categories, I asked Celia about race versus color and if the classifications themselves served as racial ones:

> KIM: Are the classifications on the *cédula* racial or color classifications?
> CELIA: Yes, and they refer to color. *Blanco, negro, indio, mestizo*, come from races.
> KIM: Are these distinct groups?
> CELIA: No . . . we are all mixed. There are no distinct groups like in the United States. You can have a Chinese and Dominican, Colombian and Peruvian, Peruvian and Chilean. There are no, as you say, groups. They come together, but there are no distinct racial groups. We are a mix.
> KIM: Some people say that color is not race—that color is descriptive. Or that Dominican, the nationality, has more to do with race than color. What is the concept of race here in the DR?
> CELIA: We start with color. *Oriental* (Asian) is *amarillo*, the Mexican is *mestizo*, the Haitian, the African, are *negro*, then there are *mulatos*—from races. We are mixed from so much immigration. There are Japanese, Chinese, Spanish, Turkish—everything you can imagine is here. There is a tremendous mixture. We Dominicans are not pure.

As I tried to tease out nationality, race, and color in this part of the interview, it was clear that race, color, and nationality are often conflated. In the Dominican Republic, Asian, Mexican, and Haitian represent both nationalities *and* races and have a particular skin color associated with them. Celia spoke about the mixture resulting from immigration, noting that Dominicans are not "pure." This was a common response in other interviews and informal discussions. The idea of purity is used to compare Dominicans with other national groups, and *indio* has most often captured this sense of mixture. *Mestizo* is also a mixed category in Mexico, and it was also used on the census in the Dominican Republic, and it was now being proposed as a category on the *cédula*.

In Brazil and Venezuela, among other Latin American countries, there is the idea that "money whitens" (Wright 1990; Twine 1998), that someone who is dark and wealthy can symbolically change his or her race or color given his or her elevated socioeconomic situation. I was in the Dominican Republic in 1998 during the homerun race between Sammy Sosa and Mark McGwire and had the opportunity to talk about Sammy Sosa as a symbol of Dominican pride with regard to issues of race, color, and class. Despite his wealth and international fame, many people still defined him as *oscuro* (dark). Celia also echoed this sentiment:

> KIM: Can money change a person's classification? Does money whiten?
> CELIA: Here no. You may be a millionaire, but if you are *prieto* (dark), you are *prieto*. You cannot change your color.

While a common color designator, *prieto* is often a derogatory term evoking an image of being dark and unattractive. At the same time, it can simply mean "very dark." Color appears to be more of a permanent category while social class is something that can change. Color becomes an important part of identity where people have learned how to classify themselves and others based on skin color, hair texture, and other facial features. Much of what Celia said here in the above interview was also expressed by other officials of the JCE. What follows here is an ethnographic account of my visits to the Junta Central to observe the cedulazation process.

The Cedulazation Process

When the cedulazation began, there was a rush to obtain the new *cédula*. Trying to beat the crowd, a close family friend went early and later commented, "The line was down the street. It was hot, and no one was selling water or anything to drink so I came home." I went to the Junta Central Electoral in Santiago on the second day and found a line of people extending out of the main door of the building and onto the sidewalk. In many ways, it was a frenzied process with extremely long lines and delays, and it was common to wait in line for six to eight hours just to get to the courtyard outside of the building where the *cédulas* were being issued. When directed by police officers who facilitated the movement of people into the building, the once single line became two distinct lines of men and women as people entered the courtyard that led to the entrance of the building. At one point, there were approximately two hundred to three hundred people waiting outside in line in the courtyard without much else to do. In extreme heat and, at times, rain, people had no choice but to wait outside until they were finally instructed to enter the building by the police officers guarding the main doors.

On the first day I observed the process, there were two police officers guarding the entrance. As days passed and the lines grew longer, more police gathered (some with batons), keeping lines straight and maintaining gendered lines in the courtyard. I took a taxi to the Junta Central Electoral and couldn't help but notice the winding line around the corner. In order to make my way to the building and into the area where the *cédulas* were being processed I had to pass at least one hundred people standing in line. I eventually made my way to the courtyard and to the front of the line by repeatedly excusing myself and assuring people that I was not cutting in front of them to obtain a new *cédula*. Once I got to the front of the line, I approached one of the police officers and asked for Celia. I explained that I was there to observe the process and that I had permission to be alongside Celia. He told me that Celia was on break and asked me to wait for her. Everything seemed to be at a standstill. I turned around, and it seemed like everyone was looking at me. I did not want to draw unnecessary attention to myself, but I became more aware of my large book bag as it became heavier on my shoulder, and I felt the need to introduce myself to people who were immediately behind me.

As I waited for Celia, I talked to Maria, who was next to me in the women's line. She told me that she resided in Miami and was in Santiago visiting family and decided to get the new *cédula* while she was there. Still thinking that *indio* had been removed as a color category on the *cédula*, I asked Maria what she thought about that, and she responded by saying that "*indio* does not exist. It was invented in the Dominican Republic." She then said, "*Indio* loses its meaning in the United States because everything is painted in black and white there."

Around this time, Celia was making her way back to the side building to enter the cedulazation area. As she approached, she introduced me to the police officer and let him know that I had permission to be there and could come back at any time to observe the process, which proved to be very help-

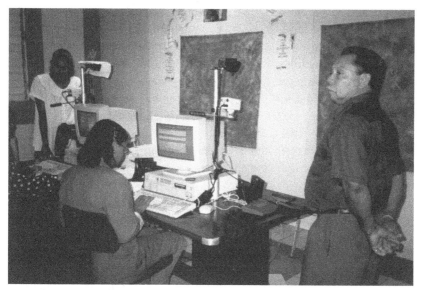

Figure 2.1. Inside the Junta Central Electoral, Santiago (*cédula* application process). Photo by the author.

ful during subsequent visits. I entered with Celia and continued my conversation with Maria when she finally entered the room.

The room was set up with a lot of hi-tech equipment such as computers, cameras, printers, and bright lights with space for about twenty people at a time. After waiting outside in line, people then had to wait in another line inside the building; this time, they were seated against the wall until they were motioned to come over to an open station. Usually, there were seven open stations at any given time where people could either renew or apply for a new *cédula* (fig. 2.1). After Celia introduced me to other staff members in the room (letting them know that I had permission from the secretary to observe the process) I sat next to Aaron, who showed me the color categories as he issued a *cédula*.

Again, based on the discussion that I had with Celia previously, I thought that the "official" *cédula* color categories were going to be *blanco, negro, mulato, amarillo,* and *mestizo* (replacing *indio*) because she had indicated that the staff had been advised of this change in their training session. Despite what they were told, and despite efforts to remove it, *indio,* in fact, remained on the *cédula,* and Celia did not know it had not been removed until she issued the first *cédula.* The five color categories were *blanco, indio, mulato, negro,* and *amarillo. Indio* remained, and *mulato* was introduced. What was the difference between the two of these categories, I wondered?

I watched as Aaron motioned to a woman to come to his station—she sat directly in front of us facing the computer. She had very light skin with light hair and blue eyes. As Aaron entered some of her personal information, such as her phone number and address, he told me that the color categories were problematic and that they do not always accurately describe the person's color. He then said, "Take her, for example, how would you classify her? Is she *blanca* or *india*? She does not fit in either category." Over time, I came to understand the categories, in part because I was defined by many Dominicans as *india clara* and by others as *mulata*. It is a complex naming process involving not only skin color, but also hair color and texture, as well as eye color (Candelario 2007, 2001). To me, the woman was not *blanca*, but she was not dark enough in combination with her hair and eye color to be *india*. As Aaron and I discussed the woman's color, he then asked her if she considered herself to be *blanca* or *india*, and without hesitation, she said, "*India*, put *india*." He commented that he was about to classify her as *blanca*.

After her *cédula* was processed, Aaron commented that there should be other categories that more closely described a person's color since there are no variations of *indio* used on the *cédula* such as *indio claro* or *indio oscuro*; *indio* represents a range of possibilities. He suggested that *trigueño* (wheat color) would have captured the woman's color more accurately, more than *blanco* or *indio*. *Trigueño* is a term that people use in daily expressions to refer to someone who is in-between *blanco* and *indio*. The next woman who was motioned to Aaron's station was dark-skinned with shoulder-length thick black hair. Again, Aaron turned to me and said that she did not really fit into any of the categories. For him, the woman was darker than *india* and almost *negra*, so he chose *mulata*. For whatever reason, unlike the woman before her, this woman did not have an option as to what her color would be even as Aaron struggled to define her according to the five color options. When I asked him if people could choose their color category, he said that they could define themselves in terms of color, but the *cédula* official had to agree with that self-definition—an example of identities needing to be affirmed.

Shortly after Aaron processed the *cédula* of the woman he classified as *mulata*, another woman came to his station. He classified her as *india*, but upon seeing her photo on her new *cédula*, she wanted to retake the picture, using more light. "I look too dark, like a 'Haitianita' (little Haitian girl) in my picture." When I asked her what she meant by "Haitianita," she said, "My pictures are usually "más clara" (lighter), and I look too dark in this picture."

Already working with another person, Aaron did not retake her photo, so she left, unhappy, having to settle with her new *cédula*.

I wondered if the woman Aaron classified as *mulata* knew that she had been defined in that way since they never entered into any discussion of her color. Since *mulato* was a new *cédula* category, I wondered what the impact would be of people being classified as *mulato* for the first time. The longer I observed the process, the more I realized that while many of the officials told me that "*indio* did not exist" and that it "really was not a color," there was still reluctance on their part to use other categories like *mulato* or *negro*. This made *indio* the default category in most of the instances unless someone was extremely light-skinned with light eyes (*blanco*) or Asian-Dominican (*amarillo*) or Dominico-Haitian (*negro*).

Observing a large number of people, with complexions ranging from light to dark being classified as *indio*, I asked Lena, another official whose station was next to Aaron's, when she would classify someone as *negro*. She responded by saying, "When someone is *negro negro*, I put *negro*." I observed her station over the next hour and never saw her use *negro* or *mulato* to classify anyone. Even when people were dark-skinned, she consistently used *indio*.

Another point is that often people did not know when their color was being recorded. They were asked for their height, date of birth, marital status, occupation, and blood type (if known). The JCE official recorded both gender and color; the category for color appears as "piel" (skin) on the *cédula*. For color, the official often looked out from behind the computer to glance at the person before classifying him or her.

If people had major changes or if they needed to provide additional documentation, their *cédulas* had to be processed in another center and picked up another day. If people were simply renewing their *cédulas* with more or less the same information, their *cédulas* were processed in the room, and they could receive them the same day. Before the *cédulas* were printed, people had a chance to review a proof sheet. Mainly they looked for mistakes in how their names were spelled, their addresses, and other personal information. As a result, I never witnessed anyone with a dispute over color. At the same time, color was already coded by the time the *cédula* was printed and issued (b-*blanco*, n-*negro*, i-*indio*, m-*mulato*, a-*amarillo*). However, I found that people did not always know how they were defined on the *cédula* in terms of color. For example, one man told me that, according to the *cédula*, he was *trigueño* when in actuality *trigueño* is not a category on the *cédula*. A woman told me that her *cédula* classified her as *india clara* when the *cédula* does not use *clara* (light) or *oscura* (dark). With reference to the officials, one man commented that "they just put what they want to."

I watched as one of the JCE officials classified an older teenage boy as *blanco,* and as he reviewed his proof sheet, I asked him how he defined himself. Without hesitation, he said, *"Indio."* I mentioned to him that he was classified as *blanco* on his *cédula,* and after he looked closely at the proof sheet and saw "b" (*blanco*) for color (*piel*), he went back to the processing area and asked that it be changed to *indio.*

Over time, I realized that this was the attitude of people obtaining their *cédulas,* and that the officials would simply define them however they chose to because "that is what they did." I asked Celia, in her experience, if anyone had ever insisted on one category over another, and she said that a man came in one day and wanted to change his color from *indio* to *negro* (this was the only reason he had come to obtain a new *cédula*). Agreeing with the man, she changed his color classification for him. What is unclear, however, is why the man would want to change from *indio* to *negro* given the social connotation of *negro.* As with many self-defined black and Afro-Dominicans, the *negro* category and self-definition is a form of resistance in opposition to *indio.*

Celia was the only official I observed frequently using categories other than *indio.* In fact, she tended to use *mulato* and *negro* exclusively and reiterated, "We are not *indios.* There are no *indios* here. *Indio* is not a color. It was invented here. We are *mulatos* and *negros,* so I am going to use those categories." As I sat next to Celia, I observed her consistently using *mulato* and *negro* and wondered if there would be any confrontations as people reviewed their proof sheets. While *cédula* applicants might not have realized that they were being classified as *mulato* and *negro* at Celia's station, other *cédula* officials took notice. During a staff meeting, Celia was told that she used *negro* and *mulato* too much, and she responded by saying, "That is what we are. We are not *indio."*

Celia's station became a site representing change in the face of resistance. This became apparent when an older dark-skinned man came to Celia's station wanting to renew his *cédula.* This process took about twenty-five minutes as the computer screen froze after taking his picture three different times. The situation grew to be more interesting as the man sat patiently making a few joking comments to the women around the station. Celia asked for his *cédula* number to retrieve his previous personal data. He indicated that he had moved, so Celia asked for his address and changed it in the system. When she got to the screen to choose a color, his current category was listed as *indio.* Celia looked out from behind her computer and changed *indio* to *negro* and prepared to take the picture. The screen froze when the picture didn't take.

After restarting her computer and the software program again, Celia re-entered his *cédula* number, changed the address, came to the screen with *indio* again, looked at him, changed *indio* to *mulato*, took his picture, and the screen froze again. After starting the computer again, and entering all of his personal information again, she came to the screen with *indio* for the third time, looked at him, changed *indio* to *negro*, took his picture, and the computer froze again. This was an unusual circumstance as her computer had not done that before. This time, she called her supervisor, who came over, restarted her computer as Celia walked away momentarily, sat in Celia's seat, asked the man his *cédula* number, and when prompted changed his address and other information. When he came to the color category (which still had him classified as *indio* from his previous *cédula*), he looked out from behind the computer and left him classified as *indio*, turned the lights up on high and took his picture; more light was needed for the picture to be taken. Unbeknownst to Celia, this is why the computer froze with her three attempts. The interesting part is that this man came to get a new *cédula* and was classified as *negro*, *mulato*, *negro*, and back to *indio* and never knew it.

Another interesting case was when Aaron was processing a woman's *cédula* and had difficulties because the last name she provided did not match what they had in the system from her previous *cédula*. He entered her infor-mation three times and had changed her existing classification from *indio* to *mulato*, back to *indio*, and finally *mulato* on the third attempt to process her renewal. While I observed the entire process of issuing *cédulas*, I recorded the classifications made at the different stations. In total, I observed 150 *cédula* applications (see table 2.1).

As I moved around to see how JCE officials were classifying people, the most commonly used category was *indio*. Celia told me, and others com-mented, that she consistently classified people as *mulato* and *negro*, so the numbers are actually higher than the ones I directly observed. Other JCE

Table 2.1 Cédula Color Categories, n = 150

Color Category	Women/*Hembras*	Men/*Varones*	Total
Indio	50	75	125
Blanco/White	4	6	10
Negro/Black	0	3	3
Mulato	6	6	12
Amarillo	0	0	0

officials told me that they, too, had classified people as *mulato* in certain instances, often when they were darker than *indio* but lighter than *negro*. The tension seemed to involve having both *indio* and *mulato* as categories on the *cédula*. People were in the habit of classifying, and being classified, as *indio*. Moreover, there was no consensus among the JCE officials about color. Someone who was *mulato* to Celia was still *indio* to Aaron. A person's official classification depended on the station to which he or she was directed. If we think about identities and categories being truly relational, the definition of light or dark could vary depending on the person doing the defining and what his or her color is.

This is also the case among African Americans in defining who is light-skinned and dark-skinned. In college, a friend who was dark-skinned described another friend of ours as light-skinned, but to me, the friend was brown-skinned, not light-skinned. In my African American culture class, I talk about the politics of skin color, naming, and identity with the students. I have noticed, inside and outside of the classroom, that one of the first descriptions that African American students give when talking about someone else who is also African American is color: "She/he is light-skinned" or "She/he is dark-skinned" are typical descriptions. "Brown-skinned" is also a common descriptor of color. Along with height (short or tall), build, and hair, color is a characteristic that is often used to define other people.

I have facilitated photo exercises in the Dominican Republic and in the United States (in class) in which participants try to "pinpoint" and describe someone's color. In the Dominican Republic, with this particular exercise, I had a small research sample of twenty people to see if there was consensus about color and the informal and formal categories. I spoke with people individually and in small groups to see if they came to an agreement about a person's color or not. I used a group of photos from Dominican magazines and newspapers. The images were of Dominicans, Americans, and Europeans, but all were from local print media. There were twenty-five images in total, and I found as I talked to people about the images that there was disagreement about color, race, and nationality.

The first image was of a young woman I would describe as being brown-skinned with shoulder-length straightened hair. When I asked about her perceived color, race, and nationality, I heard diverse responses such as *oscura*, *morenita*, *india oscura*, and *morena* for color, *mulata*, *india oscura*, *hispana*, and *trigueña* for race, and *latina* and *Dominicana* for nationality. The second image was of a man I would describe as dark-brown skinned with a faded haircut (short on the sides and longer on the top) with curly waves. When I asked about his color, I heard responses such as *oscuro*, *moreno*, and *indio*. *Latino*, *moreno*, and *mulato* were responses to race, and Brazilian and *dominicano* were responses to nationality. The seventh image was of a young man I would define as light-skinned with dark, slightly curly hair. I heard *indio* and *indio claro* for his color, *latino* and *indio* for his race, and Dominican and Dominican or Puerto Rican for his nationality. The tenth image was of a woman with long straight auburn-colored hair with highlights. There was even less consensus about her. I would define her as light-skinned. When I asked about her color, I heard *trigueña*, white-looking, *blanca*, *amarilla*, and *rubia*. For her race, I was told *latina* and *blanca*, and for nationality, I was told that she "could be a lot of things," including Venezuelan, Dominican, Mexican, American, Colombian, and Latina. If there was this much variation among people looking at still images and trying to decide what color, race, and nationality to assign, it must have been just as difficult for the JCE officials to determine color based on their own understanding of the color categories, the range of possibilities, their own socialization and experience with color, as well as their personal sense of color and someone else in relation to them.

Returning to the cedulazation, with the officials faced with five options, including both *indio* and *mulato* representing mixture, I noticed that *indio* was the prevalent category as the proof sheets were returned to one of the officials. Of the three *negro cédulas* and the twelve *mulato cédulas*, Celia processed all but two of them. Even though there was tremendous color diversity in the processing area, *indio* was almost always the default category. I did not witness any *amarillo* categorizations during any of my visits, but I was told that the category is used for people of Asian descent and that the category was assigned. Now we turn away from the *cédula* to explore the ways in which people actually talk about color, race, and nationality and how these ideas are expressed in terms of Dominicanness.

Dominicanness, Color, and Lived Experience

CLAUDIO

I first met Claudio, a thirty-year-old taxi driver, as I was leaving the Archivo Histórico de Santiago (Historic Archives of Santiago) in the downtown district known as El Centro (the center). It was noon, and that meant going home for lunch, as most people do in Santiago. Lunch is the main meal of the day, and it is an important time for family to gather.[4] As I walked down the street, I could hear the national anthem being played over the loud speakers. All of the radio stations and department and grocery stores play the national anthem at noon. Claudio commented that this was one of the legacies of Trujillo; that everything would come to a stand-still at noon during the national anthem, symbolically unifying the nation.

The traffic out of El Centro around noon can be heavy, and I was lucky to find a taxi to get home. After I entered the car and greeted Claudio, we immediately began a conversation about the day. He was on his way to take lunch to his wife, who worked in one of the Free Trade Zone factories (Zona Franca) on the edge of Santiago. This first conversation led to an interview with Claudio and his wife as well as a focus group discussion organized by Claudio. The participants were men and the focus was on race in the Dominican Republic and in the United States using the homerun race between Sammy Sosa and Mark McGwire, in 1998, as a backdrop.

When I spoke with Claudio a few days after we met, he talked about how he almost made it to the United States to live and work:

> The land is for everyone. It should be for everyone. We have all of these borders. I went to the United States once, but they won't have me. I put my picture on my cousin's visa and made it out of the Dominican Republic, but when we landed at John F. Kennedy Airport, people were waiting for me. They took me to a room and questioned me and put me on the next plane back to the Dominican Republic. The only part of the United States that I saw was the airport. I don't know if I can go back. I was engaged to a woman who was a U.S. resident, but it did not work out. Here [the Dominican Republic], you have a life but the future is not certain, and in the United States, the future is certain but you don't have a life. I have family there, and they say that life is hard.

Claudio tried to obtain a visa at the U.S. consulate in Santo Domingo and was denied. What did it mean to have a life in the Dominican Republic with an uncertain future? We talked about this in relation to Dominicans in the United States who went to the United States because they could earn more money there, but their lives are harder, more difficult because of language, discrimination, and racism compared to life in the Dominican Republic. We soon began a discussion about race and color. He described himself as *trigueño* in terms of color and as *mulato* for race. I asked if he thought his identity would change in the United States, and he commented that if he were in the United States he would be a "person of color" and that he would continue "feeling" Dominican. This was a common sentiment in other conversations and interviews when I asked about the possibility of racial and color identity changing because of migration. People often expressed that they thought they would continue to "feel Dominican" in the United States even if other things around them changed. Claudio also expressed a common sentiment about the sun and its role in darkening someone. When I asked about skin color variation, he said that the "climate can change a person's color, making them lighter or darker." There was the assumption that Dominicans in the United States would become lighter because they traveled in a northerly direction. Setting aside the tanning effects of the sun, this was still the belief when it came to someone's "natural" skin tone.

SAMUEL

Like Claudio, Samuel was a taxi driver. When we first met, when he was twenty-eight, he had not traveled to the United States but did have family in New York City. I met Samuel through Claudio, who suggested that he would have a lot to contribute along the lines of race and nationality in the Dominican Republic. Whenever I had to travel a distance, I would typically request Claudio or Samuel. Discussing life in the United States, and Dominican-Haitian relations, Samuel commented: "My family speaks of a hard life in the United States. There is discrimination there and a problem of acceptance. Here, we don't accept the Haitians. There is racism here against them. Their color and culture are different from ours. I'm proud to be Dominican. We have merengue music and the rhythm of life although it's a small and poor country." Both Claudio and Samuel talked about life in the United States being hard for Dominicans based on some of the stories they have heard about life in Washington Heights (a neighborhood in New York City where a large number of Dominicans reside). Samuel hinted that the discrimination Dominicans face in the United States is like the discrimination that Haitians face in the Dominican Republic. When I asked him about how he defined himself, he said that he preferred to use *indio* for color and *negro* for race and followed that up by adding, "That's what I am." Samuel was one of the first people I met who defined himself as a *negro* in racial terms. I asked him about race, and he said there were *blanco*, *negro*, and *mestizo* people in the Dominican Republic and that Dominicans were the *liga* (mixture) of "negros y blancos." When I asked him about him about self-defining as *negro*, he said that he had African ancestry stemming from when Haiti and the Dominican Republic were once unified (1822–1844).

CARMEN

Seventeen-year-old Carmen was a student who worked in one of the neighborhood pharmacies (family owned and operated), and I spoke at length with her during one of my visits to the pharmacy. She echoed the sentiment of the importance of a Dominican national identity: "To me, Dominican identity is more important than color or race, but Santiago is very racist. My sister is light-skinned and is dating a dark-skinned man, and my parents don't like it at all. They don't want her dating him. He is Dominican, but a dark Dominican." She added that her parents would not change their viewpoint because they were "set in their ways." Here, Carmen presents an interesting scenario—one where a dark-skinned Dominican is associated with perhaps *being* Haitian, *looking* Haitian, or having Haitian ancestry. I found that accent is one way to determine whether a dark-skinned person is Dominican or Haitian. This worked in some instances when the person spoke Haitian Kreyol and was learning Spanish, but in cases of middle-class Haitian students at the PUCMM, this was less the case. They often spoke Spanish, Haitian Kreyol, and sometimes French and/or English. Nonetheless, the idea is that Haitians do not usually speak Spanish well, and when they do speak it well, it is with a Kreyol accent. So, when color alone does not reveal national origin language may. Carmen's point about her sister's boyfriend being Dominican but dark is revealing because it suggests that Dominicans are dark—at least as dark as Haitians.

Darkness that is associated with Haitians also has social class markers associated with it. Dark skin combined with other phenotypic features and markers of poverty also mark people as being Haitian. Just as dark-skinned people are marked as Haitian, lighter-skinned Haitians often are marked or pass as Dominican, as was the case with Jean Pierre. Before I left the pharmacy, I asked Carmen about her color and race. She described herself as *india* and said that her race was *india*. As I had done in other interviews, I asked her if she thought her racial or color identity would change in the United States, and she said that she would be very proud of being Dominican and would remain *india*. Thinking about the immigration and the early census materials, I asked Carmen about her ancestry, and she described having European, indigenous, and "Arab" ancestors. Contemplating life in the United States, and proud of her Dominicanness, she did not imagine changing her *india* identity although she acknowledged that change was possible depending on the person. As Carmen and I were talking, her mother came in, listened for a while, and commented matter-of-factly that Dominicans are "una mezcla, mestiza" (a mixture) and added that there were many blacks, "la raza negra en la frontera" (the black race near the border), and that the Dominican Republic was composed of the descendants of indigenous people, Spaniards, and enslaved Africans.

ANGELA

I met forty-four-year-old Angela on a two-hour bus ride to Santo Domingo as we sat next to each other. As I was reviewing some of the questions I had on my interview schedule, she asked me about the questionnaire and my research, and after telling her about it, she showed interest in talking about it further. Unlike some of the earlier interviewees, Angela was a college graduate and had been to the United States to visit family on various occasions. She told me, "There are two classifications of *indio, claro* (light), and *oscuro* (dark). Dominicans are *mesclados* (mixed). Unlike the United States, there are no racial divisions here. Race means color here, not nationality. *Blanco* and *negro* produce the rare color *indio*. We don't have any distinct groups here because we are a mixture. Indio is a mixture of *blanco* and *negro*, more or less a *mulato*. The majority of Dominicans are *indio*. *Indio* means color and indigenous. *Indios* are indigenous with a color between *blanco* and *negro*." The comment "more or less a *mulato*" is striking because it suggests ambivalence toward the term *mulato*. She links *indio* to indigenous people in the sense that *indio* has historical significance as we explored earlier in relation to the Taíno Indians. In this way, *indio* is also tied to a sense of being an indigenous Dominican, not an "Indian" but a person who has, through ancestral ties, had a presence in the Dominican Republic for generations and can claim this *liga*. When I asked her about ancestry, Angela defined herself as *india* with "Spanish and German background."

LISA

Lisa was a twenty-year-old business student at the PUCMM and had traveled periodically to the United States. I met her at her parents' florist shop, where she worked on a part-time basis. She told me that she had given much thought to race and color based on her own experiences in the United States and the growing presence of U.S. exchange students residing in her neighborhood with host families. She also emphasized the importance of national identity: "National identity is the most important identity. It is like a card you carry that contains everything like color and race. Color and race fall within nationality. For example, when I think about an 'American,' I think of someone who is white, blonde, and speaks little Spanish even though I know there are different types of Americans. This is the image that comes to mind. This is how we are programmed to think. When I think about a 'Dominican,' I have an image of someone who is *indio* with curly or textured hair, etc." Lisa stressed something that is key throughout this book—that national identity is constructed in a way to encompass race in so much as we are socialized to associate a particular "type" of person with a particular place even though, intellectually, we know there are different "types" of people who also comprise a nation. Lisa's perspective is also illustrative of homogenization in that differences are leveled in the imagining of a "Dominican" or an "American."

The homogenization in this case is linked to how we are socialized to think in terms of images—images that are perpetuated through the media, schools, families, and other institutions, linking race, nation, and national belonging (Simmons 2006). When I asked Lisa about her color, she defined herself as *india* and said that when she is in the United States she continues "feeling" Dominican and did not think that her Dominican or *india* identity would necessarily change if she lived there. When I asked her to define *indio* she commented that for her it is a mixture of *negro* and *blanco*, a *mulato, indio*, or *moreno*. When asked about ancestry, she declined having any European, African, or indigenous ties, claiming only Dominican ancestry. Lisa's response to the ancestry question that I raised was a prevalent one highlighting the importance of *Dominican* ancestry. Therefore, while the idea of mixture exists and is critical in defining the nation and moreover Dominicanness, the *Dominican* national identity has been constructed as one of Dominican ancestry and homeland.

LUISA

Luisa and her husband own a *colmado*, a small grocery store, in one of the neighborhoods described as a somewhat exclusive professional, (upper) middle-class neighborhood. Luisa lived in the United States (New York City) for thirteen years and returned to Santiago to live after having left the Dominican Republic in search of "a better life and more economic opportunities." She commented on being Dominican, social class, and the importance of knowing "where you come from":

> National identity is the most important as it defines where you come from. There is a difference between race, color, and nation with regard to identities just like there are different classes (middle, upper, and lower). La Zurza, where we are now, is different from Pequin. Pequin is a marginalized community. People in the lower class have to send their kids to public school. That is why we go there [the United States] to have a better life, economically speaking. But this country [the Dominican Republic] is very good. Dominicans in the United States, even though they are there, raise their children with the same values and customs they had here in the Dominican Republic. Change depends

on the person. You don't have to change your values. Your customs stay more or less the same. Some people change because they are in search of money. They are chasing the dollar, and chasing the dollar can change you. Dominicans there [in the United States] are marked because of color. White people mark other people. For that reason, there is racism.

Along with gender and social class, I wanted to have a better sense of national, race, and color identities—how they are conflated and how they are perceived and lived in different ways. Again, here with Luisa, nationality emerges as the most important identity because it links one to a particular place, a place of origin. Having lived in the United States, Luisa could express the hardships and discrimination that Dominicans face there—she clearly links this discrimination to color. In racial naming processes, the normative group often identifies and names other people in relation to themselves while they remain unmarked and unnamed. In the Dominican Republic, the normative group is *indio*, but in the United States, the normative group is white.

Another distinction that Luisa made, and was also made by other people, was that "white" in the Dominican Republic has a different meaning than "white" in the United States. The difference is that a very light-skinned person in the Dominican Republic may be defined as *indio claro*, *trigueño*, or even white in terms of color, but in the United States, white represents more of a "pure" category of people with European origins and ancestry. So the same person who is considered to be *indio claro* may be considered black in the United States because of the "one-drop rule." As we talked more about color, Luisa said that she defined herself in terms of color as *india* (a mixture of *blanca* and *negra*), and with regard to race, she defined herself as a *mestiza* with African and Spanish ancestry.

NELSA

Nelsa worked two days per week as a domestic, commuting from a semi-urban community outside of Santiago where she had no running water or telephone, and sporadic electricity.[5] She was in a consensual union with one child and had an eighth grade education. For her, life was very difficult, and it was hard to find steady work. When we talked about the significance of *indio*, she commented that it meant "another class of person" and could also mean color, indigenous, and race depending on the context. She defined herself as Dominican, with only Dominican ancestry, saying that her family never discussed having any other ancestry. She described herself as *india* (color) and *india oscura* (race) because "that is what it says" on her *cédula*.

Nelsa expressed to me that she did not know much about history and that her family did not talk much about this subject. She was the first person to say that she defined herself as her *cédula* defined her. In some of my other interviews, people indicated that the *cédula* officials simply "put what they want to," without regard to how a person defines him- or herself. On the broader issue of ancestry, Nelsa claimed Dominican ancestry, not being told of other ones. All of the interview excerpts here, while addressing racial and color and national identities, point to a sense of Dominicanness that encompasses all of these identities.

Indio and Memory

The overall reluctance to use any category other than *indio* during the cedulazation process points to a continued distancing away from the idea of African ancestry. It is in this vein that these identities have become generational and more place specific. With the playing of the national anthem at noon combined with other patriotic symbols evoking images of the Dominican Republic as homeland, it becomes clear why the national image of the Dominicans has been recast in terms of *mestizo* and gradations of *indio*.

The collective memory of Dominicans as a mixed people, being *mestizo* (on the census) and *indio* (on the *cédula*), continues to reaffirm Dominicans as a mixture, not black or white, but a combination of the two and yet quite distinct from either of them. Thus, Dominicans who are defined as white or black are on the periphery with respect to contemporary articulation of Dominicanness. Over time, with a sense of the past, Dominican peoplehood grew to be expressed as a mixed status, as definitions and meanings were created in relation to whiteness and blackness against the backdrop of "Indianness."

While this peoplehood grew out of an ideology and practice of race mixing, and what the literature refers to as *mestizaje*, *mestizaje* does not quite adequately reflect the reality of the Dominican Republic as much as *mulataje* does (as discussed in the next chapter). We have come to understand that *mestizaje* represents any race mixture in Latin America; however, in its application, it has most commonly been used to explain the specific mixture of Spanish and indigenous peoples in Mexico and Peru, for example, with the category of *mestizo* stemming from *mestizaje* in word and meaning. Thus, the scholarly reproduction of this idea, combined with the continual research focus on the specific Spanish-Indian Native American mixture, has to some degree contributed to the invisibility of people of African descent in Latin American in the theorization of mixture (Minority Rights Group 1995). That is to say, when *mestizo* is evoked in the social science literature, it is not the image of an Afro-Dominican, Afro-Peruvian, Afro-Venezuelan, or Afro-Mexican. Even the definition of *mestizo* in the *Dominican Encyclopedia* reflects this notion of European-indigenous mixture. There is academic consensus along these lines. Therefore, while *mestizo*, as a socio-racial term, maintains distance from African ancestry, so does *mestizaje*.

This chapter examined the ways in which the state creates and maintains racial, and in this case, color identities by assigning color categories when people apply for their identification cards. Assigning such categories is not exact, as explored here, as officials of the Junta Central Electoral had different notions of *indio*, *negro*, and *mulato*. *Indio*, as color, is embodied and carried with people as they open accounts and show proof of identity. As a national category, *indio* demarcates the Dominican Republic and especially Dominican people in relation to Haiti. In conversations with Haitian people in the Dominican Republic, I never heard of *indio* being assigned to a Haitian person, only *negro*. In all of the interviews, everyone I spoke with talked about the cultural relevance of *indio*, suggesting that the majority of Dominicans were defined in this way officially and unofficially by Dominicans who created and named color variations such as *indio claro* and *indio oscuro*, thereby reproducing the color system in quotidian ways.

Indio has found its way into Dominican pop culture. The Dominican folk singer Mery Hernández is known as La India Canela. One of her albums has the words "La India Canela" featured prominently on the cover, and there are two songs on the album with *indio* in the title: 1) "Las Indias de Baní" (The Indias of Baní); and 2) "La India y Su Acordeón" (India and Her Accordion) (fig. 2.2). In addition, "La India Canela" is written on her accordion. Mery is light-skinned, and she recasts "india" and claims it as her stage name, thus promoting Dominicanness on both national and international levels as a recording artist. Another example involves a famous merengue song from the album *A Caballo*, produced and performed by Kinito Mendez. The song is entitled "Ritmo Merembe" (Merembe Rhythm) with a subtitle of "Los Indios." The song begins with steady drumming and a calling out of "los indios." In call and response style, the response is a type of ululation usually associated with Native Americans in the United States during ceremonies. This call and response continues throughout the song. I found another reference to "los indios" on our way to Haiti via Dajabón (one of the border communi-

Figure 2.2. Photo of La India Canela. Courtesy of Mery Hernández.

ties) as we passed through a town named Los Indios. These are just some of
the ways in which *indio* has been incorporated into the social landscape of
the Dominican Republic.

The next chapter examines the ways in which *indio*, mixedness, and
blackness are called into question as Dominicans travel and/or live in the
United States and as African Americans (students on the CIEE program)
deconstruct what it means to be black in a county where they are not often
defined that way. Mixedness and blackness are presented as constructions,
worldviews, and processes where racial and color categories are made, contested, and embodied within different contexts.

3

The Dominican Diaspora

Blackening and Whitening and Mixture across Borders

In addition to people and money, migration-driven nonmonetary resources
such as ideas, cultural values, fashion, and so on move daily between the two
countries: Dominican newspapers are distributed in the United States on
their day of publication, popular Dominican television series are simultaneously aired in New York and on the island, and Dominican media—print and
electronic—regularly cover Dominicans abroad. Similarly, exclusive and not
so exclusive boutiques on the island offer the latest fashions imported from
New York by small, informal traders, while Dominican stores in New York re-
tail foodstuff and other Dominican-made products. New York-based merengue bands frequently tour the island, while songs about Dominican migration
are hits in Latin discos and radio stations in the United States, on the island,
and even in Latin America.

Luis Guarnizo, "Los Dominicanyorks"

A central element of the experience of Dominican immigrants in the United
States stems from the different social construction of racial differences in the
two countries. The social construction of race in the Dominican Republic
combines elements of color and nationality.

José Itzigsohn and Carlos Dore-Cabral, "Competing Identities?"

Transnational migration often calls into question immigrants' conceptions of
ethnic, racial, and national identities. In the Dominican Republic, most people
perceive themselves as dark-skinned whites or light mulattoes; only Haitians
are considered black. The Dominican system of racial classification, labeling
people along a wide color continuum ranging from black to white, clashes
with the racial dualism prevalent in the United States. For most Dominican
migrants, who have some degree of racial mixture, the rule of hypodescent
means that they are black, nonwhite, or colored.

Jorge Duany, "Reconstructing Racial Identity"

For some time now, New York City, particularly Washington Heights, has
had the largest Dominican population outside of the Dominican Republic
(Grasmuck and Pessar 1991; Duany 1994; Hendricks 1974). In fact, "New
York" is often synonymous with the United States when mentioned in the

Dominican Republic (as in "Where are you from in New York?"). Yet, for many Dominicans, the Dominican Republic is still viewed as the homeland and the place where Dominicans' roots are. Long understood as a transnational community (Austerlitz 1997; Grasmuck and Pessar 1991; Hendricks 1974; Pessar 1996; Levitt 2001), Dominicans have made popular expressions like "More Dominican than Dominicans on the island," referencing Dominicans in the United States because of their efforts to maintain their heritage through cultural production such as merengue (the national dance in the Dominican Republic), food, and celebrations like the Dominican parade. I was in New York City in August 2007 and witnessed the Dominican parade through downtown Manhattan with Dominican flags flying in the air, on fans, and painted on people, with merengue and *bachata* music playing during the procession of the parade.

The increase in Dominican immigration to the United States was in large part because of the change in immigration policy following the dictatorship of Trujillo that allowed Dominicans to leave in great numbers. In combination with the establishment of the free trade zones throughout the country, as part of the Caribbean Basin Initiative to stimulate growth and stability in the Caribbean, the United States flooded the marketplace in the Dominican Republic with U.S. products. The U.S. immigration Act of 1965, the impact of import substitution, and the subsequent unemployment and poverty in the Dominican Republic served as motivation to leave for the United States in search of better employment opportunities (Torres-Saillant and Hernández 1998). What emerged was a Dominican diaspora and ideas here (*aquí*) and there (*allá*) as a way of talking about host and home countries.

When I visited the Museo del Hombre Dominicano (literally, the Museum of the Dominican Man) in Santo Domingo for the first time, I was struck by a wing of the museum depicting the life of Dominicans in New York City. There were two large mural-type paintings showing various aspects of the city (for example, taxi cabs, movie theaters, traffic, and people sitting on benches). These depictions reminded me of what I had heard in interviews—of life being hard in the United States. These images convey that sentiment.

Wanting to know more about the experience of Dominicans in the United States, I organized a focus group with professional men and women who had traveled to the United States. We met in Librería Cuesta, one of the bookstores in Santiago, during a weekly book club meeting to discuss race, color, and identity based on their experiences both in the Dominican Republic and the United States (figs. 3.1 and 3.2).

Above: Figure 3.1. A focus group in Santiago. Photo by the author.

Left: Figure 3.2. A focus group in Santiago. Photo by David S. Simmons.

We began our discussion with the first point of entry into the United States—U.S. Customs and Immigration. For many of the participants in the focus group, this point of entry was at John F. Kennedy Airport in New York City. One participant said, "We always get questions about *indio* on our passports and what it means since there are no Indians here in the Dominican Republic." Another participant said, "They look at us and think we have plantains, coconuts, coffee, and other food with us because we are Dominican." This was often my experience going through U.S. Customs as well. I'm often asked—when other travelers around me are not—if I am bringing these items back to the United States. The perception is that I am Dominican and have just returned from visiting family—I know this from brief conversations with customs officials. I would often watch as people on the plane with me were motioned to a search area to check bags for these items (this after they admitted bringing them along in their suitcases). For some years now, there have been signs at the airports in the Dominican Republic saying that these foods are not allowed (due to restrictions and concerns of the U.S. Department of Agriculture).

Along the lines of color, one participant said, "Some people wonder *how* I can be so light and Dominican. They ask if I'm Puerto Rican. They think all Dominicans are dark." Most of the participants in this focus group were light-skinned, and they agreed that Dominicans are thought of as darker than Puerto Ricans (even though there are dark-skinned Puerto Ricans). This statement led us to the lived experience of color in both national contexts.

These three statements highlight the impression of Dominicans in the United States. Upon reading *indio* on a passport, the customs official makes a claim not only about Dominicans' identity but also about Dominican history, practice, and race in saying that there are no Indians in the Dominican Republic. Questions about what produce travelers are carrying with them assumes that Dominicans are traveling with tropical goods because of stereotyped ideas of what it means to be Dominican. When Dominicans are thought of as darker than Puerto Ricans (and Cubans), and when light-skinned Dominicans are questioned about *being* Dominican when they travel abroad, the customs officials asking these questions demonstrate that they have conflated ideas of nationality, race, and phenotypic qualities, particularly skin color.

Emerging Transnational Identities

> Dominican identity in the United States must be understood as simultaneous-
> ly ethnic and racial, or "ethno-racial." By ethno- racial I mean that Dominicans
> are negotiating their status as racialized minorities operating in the context of
> histories and structures beyond their control, but they do so with a degree of
> agency and self-determination."
>
> Ginetta Candelario, *Black Behind the Ears*

Identities are becoming increasingly more important as people find themselves moving across regional, national, and international borders as well as
being shaped by (and shaping themselves in response to) global forces and
processes. Just as important is how people define themselves in racial and
color terms while simultaneously being defined by other people, institutions,
and states. It has been argued that global processes come to effect local actors' lives and circumstances in terms of reconceptualizing and understanding "localized" identities (Friedman 1994; Kearney 1995; Featherstone 1995;
Long 1996). Ideas like "the global" being embedded in the local (Long 1996)
continue to point to local processes within the global arena where people
renegotiate *who they are* due to new influences and ideas. Long (1996) asserts that re-localization is the end result of globalization whereby new local
social forms are either reinvented or created. This is what is taking place in
the Dominican Republic—people are returning with "new" ideas of race that
interact with prevalent ones. What takes place is a shifting of the influences,
where the ideas are remade and identities are reconfigured in response to
migration and new forms of information sharing—no longer just through
print publications, but via cable television, the internet, and e-mail.

Nations, once viewed as bounded entities, are now conceptualized as
unbounded as people cross and recross boundaries as part of an ongoing
transnational process (Basch et al. 1994). This involves multi-stranded relationships that link transnational migrants to both their society of origin
and the society of settlement (Basch et al. 1994). This "in-between-ness"
suggests that social actors maintain links with family and friends in their
home societies, which has implications for return or circular migration, migration of relatives and friends, and the flow of commodities and money
(Basch et al. 1994; Duany 1994; Georges 1990; Grasmuck and Pessar 1991;
Hendricks 1974). This in-between-ness also translates into changing and
homogenizing identities as transmigrants continue to (re)cross borders and
situate themselves in home and host societies. As immigration from Latin
American countries increased, for example, the United States found it nec-

essary to classify these migrants into a single "group" of people, resulting in a flattening of national differences. People from Latin America and the Spanish-speaking Caribbean became racialized as Hispanic (Oboler 1995) or as black because of phenotypic similarities to particular racial and ethnic groups institutionalized in the United States (Candelario 2001; Torres-Saillant 2000).

Racial Enculturation and the Embodiment of Race

Growing interactions between African Americans and Afro-Dominicans, and a growing understanding of race and the racial systems in both the United States and the Dominican Republic, contribute to how identities are being reconfigured. African Americans in the Dominican Republic and Afro-Dominicans in the United States encounter a racial dilemma—how one is racially defined within a new national context as categories are often based on the state's own definitions, series of laws, and informal ways of classifying people based on skin color, hair texture, and eye color.

The literature surrounding race mixture in Latin America and the Hispanic Caribbean focuses largely on racial and cultural whitening processes, creolization, and racial and cultural newness (Wade 1997, 1993; Winn 1992; Wright 1990; Duany 2002; Safa 2005, 1998; Yelvington 2001; Rahier 2003). Howard (2001), Sagás (2000), Torres-Saillant (2000), Candelario (2001), Levitt (2001), and others have examined the politics of race in the Dominican Republic and/or experience in the Dominican diaspora (in the United States in particular). While most of the work focusing on race in the Dominican Republic examines the cultural construction of *indio*, there is no contextualization of *indio* as it relates to *mestizo* or in terms of how *indio* connects with new ideas of *mulato*. Candelario (2007), Torres-Saillant (2000), and Aparicio (2006) explore what happens when Dominicans contemplate race in new ways given location and interactions with others, especially African Americans.

To understand better the emergence and significance of *mulato* in the Dominican Republic, we need first to consider the racial system of the United States and its historical relation to the African diaspora. For example, what happens to race and understandings of race in the Dominican Republic as a direct result of Dominicans' experiences with race, racism, and racializing practices in the United States? What impact do these experiences have on people's sense of themselves, their history, and the categories they use to define themselves? This is my point of departure in terms of interrogating race in the Dominican Republic.

Racialization in the African Diaspora

Dr. Ruth Simms Hamilton, the late pioneer of African diaspora studies, defined the African diaspora "as a global aggregate of actors and subpopulations, differentiated in social and geographical space, yet exhibiting a connectedness based on a shared history of common experiences, conditioned by and within a dynamic world ordering system" (Hamilton 2007, 10). While there are differences in processes of racialization throughout the African diaspora in terms of categories that are used to define people, there are similarities when we consider slavery and the racialized thinking Europeans used. Much of the research on slavery suggests that early European colonialists used biological notions of race to perceive and rank others; in viewing Africans as inferior they could justify slavery in the Americas. As Baker (1998), Harrison (1995), Smedley (1993), Blakey (1994), and others suggest, the idea of African inferiority during slavery was prevalent throughout the African diaspora. What did this mean for people throughout the African diaspora? There is a mapping of a shared historical experience of slavery, systems of inequality, and relationships where racialized identities were created and re-created that links people of African descent historically and contemporaneously.

While slavery was a common experience throughout the African diaspora, we also know that slavery itself was differently experienced due to English, Spanish, French, Portuguese, and Dutch approaches to plantation life. For European colonizers, as Baker states: "English colonists developed a unique ideology about human differences as institutional and behavioral aspects of slavery solidified. These changes continued into the early eighteenth century. Slavery developed throughout the Americas as a system of bondage that was unique in human history. Its primary distinctiveness rested on the fact that this form of slavery was reserved exclusively for Black people and their children" (Baker 1998, 13). In the Dominican Republic, according to Ernesto Sagás, the slaves on the eastern side of the island of Hispaniola viewed themselves and their circumstances differently vis-à-vis the slaves in the French colony to the west: "The slaves of the east considered themselves superior to the slaves of the west, by the simple fact that they possessed a Hispanic culture" (Sagás 2000, 25). Hispaniola is unique in this respect in terms of having Spanish and French colonial pasts.

Throughout the Americas, race became a way of identifying others and maintaining relations of power, establishing the foundation for the racial attitudes and racist practices that we find today as Harrison (1995) suggests. Race *looks different* as we explore definitions, laws, and experiences in the African diaspora. For example, one feature in the United States that is unique is the historic bipolar racial construction and categorization of what it means to be black and white (Davis 1991; Smedley 1993). If we contextualize racial formation, we have a better understanding of how racial categories have emerged in different national contexts. For example, in the United States, racial formation is linked to historical events that link blacks and whites, historically and contemporaneously, in the United States. What this suggests is that despite the presence and struggles of other groups in the United States, racial dynamics and identities are often still imagined as black and white, especially in the South. Much of racial discourse continues to be painted in black and white in the United States, unlike the racial discourses found in Latin America and the Caribbean, although this is changing due to discourses surrounding biraciality and multiraciality.

As Safa (1998) stated, Latin American and Caribbean countries created categories to describe the "newness" of their people as a result of mixture between European colonizers, enslaved Africans, and indigenous peoples among others. This idea of mixture is a long-standing one and is based on ideas of biological difference and inferior/superior social status much like in the United States, but the approach in Latin America and the Caribbean was different. Here, the idea was not to isolate African-descended people socially but rather to encourage intermarriage in order to "whiten" the population (Wade 1997). Racialization throughout much of Latin America and the Hispanic Caribbean found expression, on the one hand, in naturalizing notions of nationality and building nation-states, and a racial system that attached meaning and status to phenotypic differences on the other. In other words, one's sense of belonging to the nation (Anderson 1983) in the Americas is necessarily about one's own sense of race.

Racial Formation: Competing Racial Systems and the Idea of Mixture

When someone from the Dominican Republic travels to the United States and encounters a new and somewhat different racial system, what happens? When racial categories, once understood and accepted, are now called into question, what is the impact? Similarly, what happens when a self-defined black person from the United States travels to the Dominican Republic and is all of a sudden defined as *indio*? When people encounter new racial systems they have to negotiate "who they are" and what they are perceived to be within this new context. This often involves making sense of the categories and racialization in that particular place.

From 2000 through 2004, I had the unique opportunity to direct a study abroad program in Santiago, Dominican Republic, through the Council on International Educational Exchange (CIEE). The program focused on Spanish and Caribbean studies. Over four-and-one-half years, different groups of U.S. college students came to spend a semester in the Dominican Republic. This program attracted many African American and Latino/a students because of its location and programmatic theme (Simmons 2008, 2006, 2001). Many African American students came to learn about another country and culture in the African diaspora, and Dominican American and other Latino/a students chose the program to learn more about their culture and heritage. Each semester, similar patterns emerged surrounding issues of race, identity, and what it meant to be American, black, and/or Dominican (Simmons 2008, 2006, 2001). Depending on skin color (combined with hair texture and style), African American students were often thought of as having Dominican or Haitian ancestry while Dominican and other Latino/a students were often defined as Dominicans "de allá" (from there—the United States) because they were somewhat "Americanized." White students were publicly called "Americanos," "rubios," or "gringos," and many of them shared with me that they had to contemplate their whiteness and Americanness for the first time. Asian American students (Japanese, Filipino, and Chinese) were grouped together under the informal Dominican Asian category "chino" (Chinese), while Indian American students (whose parents were from India) were classified as "hindu" despite their religious affiliations. This had an impact on the students because all of a sudden they were defined by other people with unfamiliar categories. Many of the students felt uncomfortable about these perceptions (Simmons 2006). An indirect—and perhaps direct—result of their time abroad in the Dominican Republic prompted many of the students to question their previously held ideas about their own racial identities.

Students attempted to understand and make sense of the racial/color categories that Dominicans used to define not only them but also themselves. African American students understood and lived race differently in the United States and wanted to know why Dominicans were "in denial" as evident to them by the everyday usage of *indio* (Simmons 2008, 2006). For African American students, Dominican *had to be black*, and their apparent refusal to accept this frustrated many of the students. They wanted to know how it was possible for someone to reject *being black*—to reject their history and ancestry—and not accept *who they were*. I explained that *black*, as a category, and pride in being black is a process, a journey—that racialization is a process by which we come to understand and internalize racial definitions and concepts developed through particular historical and cultural processes

(Simmons 2006). This was not good enough for the students. By this point in the students' lives, they had a very firm sense of themselves and an identity that was, in many ways, unquestioned. They *were black*, but many of them did not have an opportunity to reflect on being black and the process by which they actually *became black*—that is until now.

The black students often commented, "but they look like us," ranging from light to dark in skin tone. What the students were learning was that Dominicans had come not only to see themselves as mixed but also to label that mixture with color terms. Again, African American students were used to skin color terms, but it was the *indio* designator that was unsettling to them because it suggested that Dominicans were claiming an indigenous past and identity while negating their blackness. In class and in discussion groups with the students, we talked about historical mixture in both contexts.

While the Dominican Republic encouraged and *practiced* ideas of mixture through miscegenation and whitening practices, the United States had similar intermixture during the colonial period but later discouraged it and had laws prohibiting intermarriage. As in other countries, miscegenation did occur in the United States during slavery, but this mixture represented a type of gray area, especially in the early twentieth century as mulattos *became* black in 1920. Before this time, quadroon, octoroon, and mulatto were used categories and captured the idea of African or black blood or ancestry. So, what this means for the students is that their generation and that of their parents and grandparents were defined as black and socialized to think of themselves in this way. Some of their parents and grandparents were reminded of their blackness and racial place in society because of Jim Crow laws and other structures that reinforced ideas of black and white despite skin color variation in the black community.

Thus, in the United States, people of African descent have historically been defined as black. Mixture is a given as many people who are black in the United States *are* mixed because of historical miscegenation. The term "mixed," however, is generally used for a person with direct mixed parentage in the United States. This is not the case in the Dominican Republic. Dominican mixture is expressed as being betwixt and between black *and* white—it isn't black *or* white—but rather *indio, mestizo,* and/or now *mulato*.

The similarities and differences in the racial systems of the Dominican Republic and the United States become apparent when comparing Dominicans' and African Americans' racial, and more particularly color, identities. African Americans in the Dominican Republic attempt to define themselves within the Dominican racial system while Dominicans in the United States are faced with yet another racial system. On both sides, people try to make sense of their own identities and sense of history within a new context where they are defined in new ways. Often, African Americans come to understand "mixed-ness" while Dominicans come to understand "blackness." What emerges is not only a new or changing sense of self and selves in the African diaspora but also a "community of consciousness," a mutual recognition of similarity, and a strategic alliance based on shared history and lived experience (Simmons 2005, 2001).

The idea of race, within particular contexts, is being reconfigured due to the interaction between external and internal forces as evidenced by changing racial and color categories and the articulation of "new" identities throughout the African diaspora. In other words, racialization and racial formation are ongoing processes depending on who is entering and leaving national borders, prompting redefinitions, changing categories, and new identities as people confront new racial systems and racial categories.

Dominicans in the United States vis-à-vis African Americans

Two popular Dominican musicians, Wilfredo Vargas and Fausto Rey, adopted afros and the cool look of New York soul and boogaloo musicians in the 1970s, when such styles still elicited scorn from both the left and the right in Santo Domingo.

Jesse Hoffnung-Garskof, *A Tale of Two Cities*

I was in the Historic Archives in Santiago in July 1995 when I came across an article in *El Siglo* entitled "Bailando con los negros" (Dancing with the Blacks).[1] What first caught my attention was the photo of Jesse Jackson I wondered if he had recently been in the country or was planning a visit. I glanced at the title, which made me all the more interested in the article, and I wanted to know what "dancing with the blacks" meant and "who was black" in this context. The article is about Dominicans and African Americans coming together during a Fourth of July celebration in New York City in 1995. Urbáez, the writer, describes the shared social space, good time, food, and music, but more important is the discussion of race as experienced in the United States:

Compartiendo con aquellos negros, . . . comprendimos más los intereses y los sentimientos de los negros norteamericanos, que contrario a muchos de nosotros, nacionalistas postizos, se sienten orgullosos de ser negros, de sus costumbres y tradiciones, incluidas sus diferentes manifestaciones de religiosidad. . . . Creemos que tanto Peña como Leonel Fernández, porque allá todo mulato es "negro," deberían acercarse a la comunidad negra norteamericana en busca de recursos y apoyo a sus aspiraciones. (Urbáez 1995)

(Sharing with the blacks, . . . we understand the interests and feelings of North American blacks, which are contrary to many of us, in that they feel proud of being black, of their customs and traditions, as well as different manifestations of religiosity. . . . We believe that Peña [Gomez, a candidate in the Dominican presidential election] as well as Leonel Fernández [another candidate] should become closer to the North American black community in search of resources and to support their aspirations because all mulattos are black there [in the United States].)

These sentiments were published in a newspaper in the Dominican Republic and represent the flow of information about race and the experience of African Americans and Dominicans in the United States. There is recognition of "sameness" and "difference" in this piece in the statement that "all mulattos are black there" (in the United States), suggesting that mulattos are *not* black here (in the Dominican Republic). At the same time, there is the idea that Dominicans could benefit by allying themselves with African Americans in the United States in terms of resources and opportunities. Urbáez, the journalist, writing for a Dominican audience in the Dominican Republic, informs his readers that Dominicans participated in this Fourth of July celebration with African Americans, whom he defines as "*negros*." Importantly, Urbáez conveys a sense of lived experience in the United States and the idea that Dominicans *soon understand* that black Americans are proud to be black, "unlike them."

Urbáez also suggests that both Peña Gomez (*negro*) and Leonel Fernández (*mulato*) are black in the United States and that much could be learned and gained by Dominicans and African Americans joining forces. This article is an example of a transnational project, and more specifically, transnationalism embedded in the "local" as Dominicans in the Dominican Republic learn of the experiences of Dominicans abroad, and in particular about changing ideas of race and community building. Of note, there was no mention of Jesse Jackson in the piece, just his picture. I later realized that Jesse Jackson has served as a symbol of the African American community in Dominican media. This is changing, however, with the presidency of Barack Obama.

el roedor

Por Aristófanes Urbáez
Sub-Editor de Cultura y ¡Diversión!

Bailando con los negros

"¡Negros del continente: al Nuevo Mundo/ habéis dado la sal que le faltaba!".

Jesse Jackson

Una de las experiencias más gratas que hemos disfrutado en nuestra vida, fue el atrevimiento que tuvimos de meternos en una fiesta al aire público que tenía el Centro Comunitario Wilson Robinson, de la comunidad negra, en la calle 148 en el condado de Harlem, en la ciudad de Nueva York. Luis González Peña, Juanito Lora, Catarey Alvarado, Ramón Urbáez, quien suscribe y nuestro hijo Ivén, de 11 años, departimos por espacio de dos horas con aquellos negros chulísimos que les dicen a todos los dominicanos "Papi". Disfrutamos de un banquete todo gratis, de su música con profundas raíces africanas, incluidas más de 100 jaibas sancochadas que degustamos de una obsequiosa negra gorda que nos las regalaba con una gran sonrisa blanca como la nieve. Compartiendo con aquellos negros, que celebraban al igual que los blancos, la Independencia de su país, los Estados Unidos, una barrera de prejuicios rodaron por el suelo y comprendimos más los intereses y los sentimientos de los negros norteamericanos, que contrario a muchos de nosotros, nacionalistas postizos, se sienten orgullosos de ser negros, de sus costumbres y tradiciones, incluidas sus diferentes manifestaciones de religiosidad. Ningún norteamericano negro —ahora lo sabemos más que nunca— se cambiaría por un blanco, porque en la negritud está su raza, su cultura y la fuerza de sus raíces. ¡Qué grata experiencia! Creemos que tanto Peña, como Leonel Fernández, porque allá todo mulato es "negro", deberían acercarse a la comunidad negra norteamericana en busca de recursos y apoyo a sus aspiraciones.

Al Doctor Peña Gómez

Pedro Corporán

El licenciado Pedro Corporán (que es Licenciado de verdad, no postizo), es uno de los dirigentes más serios y de más valía que tiene el PRD en la comunidad de Nueva York. Serio, trabajador, estudioso, lector voraz, Pedro Corporán jamás ha estado ligado al bajo mundo, sino a actividades legales que comenzaron con la compra de automóviles en subastas los cuales revendía para subsistir. Como muchos otros dominicanos provenientes de las izquierdas, Corporán se integró al proyecto Peña Gómez porque cree en él (y esta conclusión la hemos sacado de conversaciones en que de manera respetuosa ha expresado sus juicios acerca de la historia y los políticos dominicanos). A pesar de su juventud, Corporán, quien es además columnista de *El Nacional* y tiene un programa sabatino de televisión en Nueva York que se denomina "Entrega Especial", es ampliamente respetado por quienes le conocen por la seriedad con que realiza su trabajo. Y esto se lo decimos a Peña nosotros, que ni somos perredeísta, ni empleado asalariado de Pedro Corporán. Y lo hacemos por una razón: hay que desterrar el odio, el chisme y la cizaña del alma de todos los dominicanos, sin importar los partidos en que militen. ¡Tómenos la palabra, señor Peña Gómez!

Figure 3.3. A photo of Jesse Jackson in an article in *El Siglo* in 1995. Courtesy of the Archivo Histórico de Santiago.

So, what happens to *indio* when Dominicans experience the U.S. racial system? The closest term to *indio* in the United States is mulatto in connoting black-white mixture. The term *indio* is problematic in the United States because when translated *indio* means "Indian" or "indigenous," and since Dominicans are not considered to be Native American or from India, it is often challenged. However, mulatto is not always the most appropriate category for Dominicans to claim either. Not only is it no longer a racial category in the United States since all mulattos legally became black in 1920, but it is often viewed as an impolite, insulting, and negative term. Mulattos were *turned into blacks* in the United States, in part, to create and maintain racial segregation, to define people of African descent in the same way, under one racial umbrella, because of mixture. Therefore, the black, or African American, community is composed of people who resemble Dominicans in many ways—from light to dark—with parallel experiences with intra-group naming (colorization), marrying up, lightening creams, hair straighteners, and other cultural practices.

In 1993, the Dominican-born writer Julia Alvarez wrote about her personal experiences with skin color in the Dominican Republic in *Essence*, a magazine with a predominantly African American women's audience: "All of us aspired to be on the lighter side of the spectrum. Don't get me wrong. None of us wanted to be white-white like those pale, limp-haired gringos, whites who looked as if they'd been soaked in a bucket of bleach. The whiter ones of us sat out in the sun to get a little color *indio*, while others stayed indoors rubbing Nivea on their darker skin to lighten it up!" (Alvarez 1993, 42). The "lighter side of the spectrum" that Alvarez talks about reflects the politics of skin color in the Dominican Republic, which has historically involved whitening practices such as skin lightening creams and "marrying up" with the hope of lightening the next generation. This was also the case historically among African Americans in the United States. In a country where mixedness is espoused and expressed in terms of being *mestizo, indio,* and more recently *mulato,* being lighter (*claro*) is preferred to being darker (*oscuro*). Arguably, this preference still exists for some African Americans (Simmons 2008; Russell et al. 1992; Hunter 2005; and in such films as *Black Is . . . Black Ain't* [1995], *A Question of Color* [1993], and *School Daze* [1988]). Here, Nivea is a code word for a bleaching cream used to lighten one's skin tone over time. For both Dominican and African American women, in particular, the idea was that to be lighter was not only more attractive and "better," but was also attainable through bleaching efforts. Such bleaching creams were advertised in Dominican and U.S. newspapers in the early to mid-1900s and were marketed to women (and some men), claiming that they could become lighter, and in some cases, whiter (figs. 3.4 and 3.5).

Both of the ads reproduced herein show a two-toned woman—one side with darker skin and the other side with lighter skin made possible by a skin lightening cream—and suggest that the skin not only becomes lighter but also "beautiful." An earlier ad appeared in the *Chicago Defender* in 1921; it

EL CUTIS BLANCO DE PERLA ES DE VERDADERA BELLEZA

La diferencia se aprecia instantáneamente

rencia. Desde que toca el cutis se pone de manifesto un color blanco, transparente, fascinantemente aterciopelado y de radiante hermosura. Compárese el lado del rostro así preparado con el cutis natural, y ello bastará para convencerse de lo maravilloso de los resultados que se obtienen.

CREMA ORIENTAL de GOURAUD

Resulta valiosísima para el tratamiento de los barros de la cara y el cutis barroso, grasiento, marchito y fláccido. El efecto altamente antiséptico que ejerce constantemente proteje a la piel de las contaminaciones. Compre hoy mismo la Crema Oriental de Gouraud e iníciese en el secreto de una nueva belleza eterna.

Basta aplicarse la Crema Oriental de Gouraud en un lado de la cara para darse cuenta de la dife-

Ferd. T. Hopkins & Son
New York   Paris   Montreal   London

Figure 3.4. Whiteness ad in the Dominican Republic, *El Diario*, 1930. Courtesy of the Archivo Histórico de Santiago.

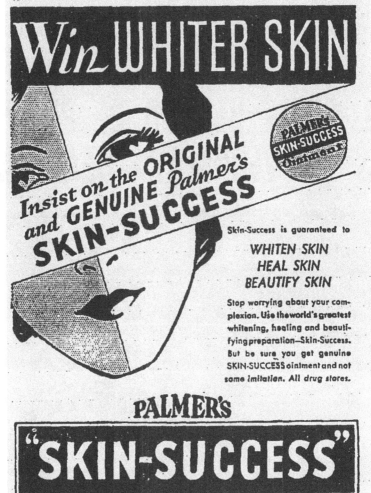

Figure 3.5. Whitening ad in the United States, *Chicago Defender,*
September 17, 1921. Courtesy of the *Chicago Defender.*

said in bold letters, "Beautiful women: You can be Beautiful too." The ad reads, "Every one [sic] naturally wants to look their best—it makes others respect, admire and love you. You owe it to yourself and your friends to look your best at all times—and here are a few suggestions for whitening the complexion, smoothing the hair and improving your looks generally." This skin whitening product was marketed for skin and hair, suggesting that the result would make women beautiful. The three women in the ad appear to be white, not black or even light-skinned black women. Ads and products like the ones here indicate a preference for lightness or near- whiteness. This ad (as well as the other one) appeared in a prominent African American news-paper in Chicago. Ads in later years linked whitening creams with social status (among the social elite) and the preferences of men (that men pre-ferred lighter-skinned women). Many of these ideas were later challenged with black authenticity claims and with "black is beautiful" cultural markers such as West African clothing, afros and short natural hair styles, and a celebration of darker skin tones. Nonetheless, the politics of skin color con-tinue to exist in the African American community (Simmons 2008), finding expression not only in skin color terms but also in childhood rhymes such as "If you're light, you're right. If you're brown, stick around. If you're black, get back."

In both the United States and the Dominican Republic, African Ameri-cans and Dominicans internalized lightening or whitening ideals over time. Marrying up was a practice in both the Dominican Republic and the United States among African Americans. Both Dominican and African American women used skin lightening creams (and some continue to do so). The above advertisements contain images of a brown-skinned woman turned light af-ter applying a whitening cream. These advertisements ran in Dominican and African American newspapers around the same time (1930–1933) in both the Dominican Republic and the United States. The idea was that lighter skin was more attractive and "better" than darker skin. These creams are still sold in pharmacies and department stores in the Dominican Republic, and I have seen similar products in beauty supply stores in South Carolina.

Mixture and the Emergence of *Mulato* in the Dominican Republic

When Dominicans enter the United States, they enter at the point of the national racial system where there are new rules and racial definitions based on the history and sociopolitical circumstances of the United States. They may encounter the color-naming practice among African Americans at some point or over time, but in general they encounter the idea of—all of a sudden—being black. For Dominicans in the United States, the people who "look like them" are not defined as *indio* or *mulato* but importantly as black and/or African American. Similarly, Dominicans find themselves being defined as black and/or Afro-Latino, and some of them start to redefine themselves in this way while creating alliances with African Americans and other black ethnic groups due to shared circumstances.

While this type of questioning and redefinition take place in the United States, it also has an impact on racial categories and identities in the Dominican Republic. The usage of *mulato* as a category on the *cédula* is just one example. Today, there are references to being *mulato* in print and television media, and the Department of Education is working with Dominican educators to rewrite history books to include more about the African presence and ancestry in the Dominican Republic.[2]

The late 1980s witnessed a shift in some of the prevailing ideas of race and ancestral claims in the Dominican Republic with the emergence of *mulato*. Migration between the United States and the Dominican Republic, experiences with other racial systems, alliances with other people of African descent in the Americas, along with new forms of communications have all contributed to a changing sense of self and selves in the Dominican Republic. In addition, Dominican scholars and activists are questioning their own socialization in terms of what they learned about *being Dominican* and about the African past. This changing racial sense translates into a new consciousness of Dominican history and place that works to situate the Dominican Republic in the African diaspora. As a result, new forms of identities have arisen—Afro-Dominican and *mulato* in particular—that (re)claim the African past, challenge earlier racial concepts, and link Dominicans with other people of African descent in the Caribbean, the United States, and throughout the African diaspora.

In May 1996, *mulataje* and blackness found expression in the presidential campaign in the Dominican Republic. The public discourse surrounding two of the candidates was both racial and national. At that time, the current president of the Dominican Republic, Leonel Fernández, representing the Partido de la Liberación Dominicana (Dominican Liberation Party, or PLD), was running for office for the first time, and his opponent was the late Francisco Peña Gomez, representing the Partido Revolucionario Dominicano (Dominican Revolutionary Party, or PRD). Prior to the election, Leonel Fernández resided in the United States, and Peña Gomez resided in Santo Domingo. Fernández was new to public service, while Peña Gomez had served as mayor of the capital city, Santo Domingo. The debate had little to do with their histories in public service and more to do with race and national origin (Sagás 2000; Howard 2001).

The discussion in print and television media advanced the idea that Peña Gomez was of Haitian descent and black while Fernández was Dominican, living in the United States, and mixed. The opposition to Peña Gomez grew as fears were generated that, if he were elected, the island would be unified again and the borders would open to let Haitians enter the Dominican Republic freely—thus a renewed fear of Haitianization ensued. Most of the accusations were traced to the outgoing president, Joaquín Balaguer, and his political party, Partido Reformista Social Cristiano (Social Christian Reformist Party, or PRSC).

After the election and the votes were counted, Peña Gomez received 41.1 percent of the votes, Leonel Fernández received 38.9 percent, and Jacinto Peynado of the PRSC received 15 percent. The remaining votes were split between other smaller political parties (http://pdba.georgetown.edu/Elecdata/DomRep/drpr196.html). Because none of the three candidates had received a majority vote, a second-round election was initiated with Balaguer and the former president Juan Bosch (PLD) endorsing Fernandez. The "run- off," or second round, election took place on June 30, 1996 between Peña Gomez and Fernández with Fernández winning 51 percent of the votes and Peña Gomez winning 49 percent; Fernández won the election by a slight margin.

There were two currents running through the election campaign. The first was when Balaguer and others linked Peña Gomez to Haiti, defining Dominicanness along the lines of race and national belonging, and tried to create fear among voters. The second current was when Dominicans, despite the racialized context during the election, voted for Peña Gomez in large numbers during both elections. Before the election, Fernández commented about the issue of race in the election. In a *New York Times* article on July 1, 1996, Fernández is quoted as saying, "This is not some competition between Robert Redford and Nelson Mandela . . . Look at me. I myself am not white. The population in this country is predominantly mulatto, and I too am a mixture of white and black. So how can anyone talk of a racist campaign?" (Larry Rohter, *New York Times*, July 1, 1996, p. A3). Claiming to be mixed—black and white—Fernández linked himself to the majority of Dominicans in the country whom he defined as *mulato*.

It is striking that it was during Fernández's first term as president that *mulato* first appeared on the *cédula*, making this the first time that a mixed category implying African ancestry would be used as an official state-sanctioned category in the Dominican Republic (since the first national census in 1920). In everyday discourse, *mulato* is gaining popularity in part because of the ways in which returning migrants and their children talk about their experiences in the United States along with media and pop-culture descriptions of Dominicans and their relationships with other groups in the United States.

Torres-Saillant and Hernández (1998, 157) address the issues surrounding racism in the United States:

> Ironically, it is neither the unskilled nor blue-collar workers who most dramatically suffer the oppressive weight of racial discrimination. Their own social segregation, their confinement to labor markets populated mostly by their own people, keeps them for the most part from stepping outside their immediate ethnic milieu. As they hardly ever get to interact with people from the dominant sectors of society, they stay largely away from the settings where the drama of racism can be felt directly. It is really the professionals and those most qualified to compete for employment, education, and commercial opportunities in the mainstream who feel it in their flesh. It is they who get the chance to experience personally the extent to which their phenotype can limit their aspirations.

While Dominicans in general may experience some forms of racism in the United States, Torres-Saillant and Hernández suggest that it is the middle class or at least those individuals with human and social capital that most often confront racism. I believe it is for this reason that we find more Dominicans entering into civil rights organizations such as the NAACP as well as African American sororities and fraternities in U.S. colleges and universities. The issue of social class is also interesting here in that Torres-Saillant and Hernández suggest that early studies (for example, Grasmuck and Pessar 1991; Georges 1990; Hendricks 1974) relied primarily on ethnographic studies of small communities in the Dominican Republic and suggested that the post-1965 Dominican migrants to the United States were primarily rural, uneducated, poor, unskilled, and jobless (Torres-Saillant and Hernández 1998, 34). They argue instead that most migrants actually came from the urban middle class, and were neither poor nor uneducated. They were Dominican doctors and other professionals who became entrepreneurs to supplement their incomes in the United States because of practices that kept them from fully participating in their professions without further training and education. This connects with the earlier discussion on the middle class being confronted with racist practices in the United States (alongside others without as much social and human capital).

Ong's (1996) discussion of "blackening" and "whitening" is relevant here. It appears that Dominicans, despite educational level and professional preparedness, are subjected to blackening processes in the United States. During her visit to Michigan State University in 1999, the Dominican sociologist Ramona Hernández suggested, during her talk, that Dominicans in the United States do not follow the same trajectory as other Latinos because they tend to be darker.

Ana Aparicio (2006, 138) suggests that the idea of blackness is changing for second-generation Dominicans in the United States: "The identity issue that most second-generation Dominicans engage with is 'what kind' of Black identity they embody. That is . . . many people I worked with feel that others tried to pressure them to make a choice between being Dominican and Latino or being Black. They do not see the two as separate but feel that Black friends would often urge them to identify themselves as Black. . . . They acknowledge membership in the Black diaspora, but they infuse this with Latino or Dominican elements of identity."

Ginetta Candelario (2001, 69), comparing the experience of Dominicans in New York City and Washington, D.C., with regard to blackness, suggests: "These Dominicans [in Washington, D.C.] identify as black nearly twice as often as often as Dominicans in New York City precisely because the Dominican community in D.C. is small, has origins in West Indian and U.S. origin African-American communities in the Dominican Republic, took root in a segregated Southern city, and came in age in the midst of a large, economically and politically diverse African American community."

Both Aparicio and Candelario talk about Dominicans' experience with African Americans as friends and as being part of the same community. These relationships play an important role in Dominicans' navigating the racial terrain of the United States where they are perceived to be black as well as Latino/a.

Blackening and whitening processes also occur in the Dominican Republic under the terms Dominicanization and Haitianization as people cross the border and enter the Dominican Republic. Every time I travel to the Dominican Republic, I have a similar experience at the airport upon arrival. In 1995, with my U.S. passport in hand, I was asked questions about being Dominican and coming back to the island (that is, what I was bringing for family, if I was born "there" with roots "here," and so forth). During one trip, as I left the customs area and exit doors of the airport, I noticed a group of college-aged students from the United States. An African American student seemed upset about something. I walked over to the group, said hello, and spoke to him in particular. He looked at me and said, "They think I'm Haitian. When they saw my U.S. passport, and noticed that I spoke English, they said that I must be Haitian American." Before leaving the airport that day, we were both defined and labeled—him as a Haitian and me as a Dominican. We were both dressed in a similar fashion, spoke English, and held U.S. passports. Our color set us apart. Because he was dark-skinned, he was defined as a Haitian American, and because I am light-skinned, I was defined as Dominican American.

In 1999, Anthony, an African American student studying in the Dominican Republic, was detained at the border overnight when he and some Haitian friends decided to visit Haiti for the weekend. Having accepted the invitation to visit his friends' family across the border from Dajabón about two hours from Santiago where he was studying, Anthony and his friends had crossed the border into Haiti without incident, but a problem arose when they tried to return to the Dominican Republic on Sunday. The border was closed. However, with Haitian passports in hand, along with their Dominican visas, Anthony's friends were prepared to pay a nominal fee to enter the Dominican Republic. Unlike his friends, Anthony did not carry his passport with him and could not establish his citizenship at the border. Anthony was dark-skinned and thought to be Haitian, which made his case even more difficult to prove. In that moment, to the border officials, he became an undocumented Haitian trying to cross the border into the Dominican Republic. The officials did not believe that he was an American student studying in the Dominican Republic. As a result, he had to spend the night in a building on the border until the border officially opened the next day. Early Monday morning, Anthony contacted the office of the Council on International Educational Exchange (CIEE) office in Santiago, and someone from the staff faxed a copy of his passport to border officials prompting his immediate release, and he traveled back to Santiago without further incident.

In 1998, I made this same trip with close Dominican friends and my family, and my experience was quite different. We were invited to visit our friend's brother in Dajabón over the weekend and to go to Haiti for the day on Sunday, the day the border is officially closed. My husband (David), our oldest daughter (Asha) who was one year old at the time, and I are all light in complexion. Our friends said that we would cross the border as Dominicans and that there was no need to bring our passports; "Dominicans do not need them," they said. They also suggested that we not have conversations with people because our Spanish would make people wonder if we were "de allá" (the United States). If asked, they would say that we were their cousins visiting from the United States. This was our first trip to Haiti, and I was a bit nervous given the situation of not having our passports and the border being closed.

As we approached the border, there was someone inside at a desk. One of our friends told the official that we wanted to visit Haiti for the day. The border official gave all us slips of paper and we were allowed entry into Haiti. As we crossed the bridge connecting the Dominican Republic and Haiti, the only marker delineating the two countries was a link chain from one side of the bridge to the other. There was no sign indicating that we were in Haiti, but as we stepped over the chain, I realized that we must have crossed the border. When we reached the other side of the bridge in Haiti, we were in Ouanaminthe and were met with a few transportation options. We got into a truck and traveled through the town. We later asked the driver if there was an art gallery where we could purchase Haitian art. After we left the art gallery, we returned to the border to cross back into the Dominican Republic.

Earlier in the day, we crossed without incident, but now as we stepped back over the same chain, we were faced with a large cement structure ahead that read "República Dominicana" (Dominican Republic). I looked back toward the Haitian side and saw only people, trees, trucks, and motorcycles as we walked in the direction of an imposing border symbol. A Dominican man greeted us as we stepped back over the chain and began a conversation with me. I recalled what our friends had said about not talking (that my Spanish was not "Dominican Dominican"), but the man didn't say anything about my Spanish. He simply led us to the processing area where we returned our slips of paper, paid a nominal fee, and entered the Dominican Republic as Dominicans.[3]

I heard Anthony's story for the first time when I became the resident director of the CIEE Study Center in Spanish Language and Caribbean Studies in Santiago in January 2000. The previous director recounted the story and commented that since that incident she had encouraged the African American students to carry copies of their passports with them as proof of U.S. citizenship. More to the point, she asked them to carry their passports to prove that they were not Haitian. I wondered what the students thought about this suggestion, especially in a country where many of them felt a connection to place, because the Dominican Republic is part of the African diaspora (Simmons 2006, 2001). The CIEE had a practice of faxing copies of all of the students' passports to the U.S. embassy to register them as Americans in the country; this was actually the practice of all CIEE programs worldwide, but the African American students were the only students encouraged to carry a copy of their passports with them. White, Latino/a, and Asian American students were not told to carry a copy of their passports.

As the director, I later made the suggestion that all students carry a copy of their passports with them as another form of identification, in part, so that the African American students would not be singled out in orientation. I was also careful not to predict their experiences: I did not suggest that Dominicans would think that the U.S. students were Haitian because of their color, and in some cases, because of their natural or braided hair (Candelario 2007, 2000). Braids are usually associated with Haitian women, and many of the African American women students wore braids, had short natural hairstyles, or wore their hair in natural curly locks. Dominican women, in contrast, tend to wear their hair in straight relaxed style (Candelario 2007). This is changing, however, especially among the younger generation with experience in the United States among African Americans and other people of African descent.

I was also careful not to predict their experiences because some of the African American students were lighter in complexion, and even with natural hair styles they would not be thought of as Haitian. It was only the darker-skinned students, with and without natural hair styles, who were often marked as Haitian. So, while some of the African American students were thought of as Haitian, others were not. For this reason, I did not want to tell students what *would* happen but rather what *could* happen based on the previous experiences of other students. In the Dominican Republic, there is a practice of referring to people in public by using skin color categories (such as *morena* or brown) to get their attention; this is the case when the person's name is not known. It is common to hear, for example, "ven aquí morena" (come here brown girl) while walking down the street. Other terms such as "gringo/a" or "rubio/a" (blonde) were used if the students were perceived to be American or had blonde hair. Through a culmination of experiences over the course of the semester, students called their whiteness, blackness, Latino(a)ness, and Americanness into question as new questions arose about the significance of these categories and identities in the Dominican Republic.

During workshops and discussions with students, I was always struck by the comment that "Dominicans are confused about who they are . . . they don't know that they are black." I tried to respond to this statement by asking the students to step back and consider the historical context and socialization practice (Simmons 2006). My response that Dominicans did not learn that they were black did not seem to satisfy the students because they could not understand how it was possible that people who *looked like them* could not see themselves as black (as they did). There is a segment in the *Mirrors of the Heart* video that discusses the politics of skin color, "good" and "bad" hair, marrying up in the Dominican Republic, and where a Dominican poet and proponent of Afro-Dominicanness, Blas Jiménez, says, "We haven't been able to grasp our negritude yet." Students tended to react strongly to the ideas expressed in the video. When I said, "This is similar to what happened in the United States among African Americans years ago," they looked at me in disbelief. For many of them, they were proud to be African American, proud of their history, and proud of what it meant to them to be black, but they did not think about the processes and movements that facilitated that kind of pride. I told them about the historical preference for lightness, about people who chose to define themselves as mulatto instead of black, about skin lightening creams in the United States, about "good" and "bad" hair, and about marrying up as a strategy to lighten the next generation. Many of the students could identify with, and have experienced, the politics of skin color and colorization practices of naming—marking light to dark skin tones—as well as "good" and "bad" hair, but they were often surprised to learn about the other points of similarity.

After students had been in the country for one month, we had another meeting, similar to a retreat, to discuss the students' experiences overall and to learn about their classes and homestays. Some of the *estudiantes de apoyo* (support students/peer group) also attended this meeting. Students were settled at this point and could reflect and speak openly about their experiences, any culture shock, and what they were learning. During this meeting, we allowed students to speak in English so that they could express themselves fully (most other interactions between students and CIEE staff were in Spanish per the CIEE language policy). It was during this meeting that we learned more about their racialized experiences, perceptions of Dominican culture, and incorporation into Dominican life. Some of the African American women students commented that their host mothers invited them to go to the salon to get their hair *done*, which meant straightening their hair. While some of the students wore their hair straight and thus frequented Dominican salons, other students with braids and natural styles took the suggestion to mean that something was *wrong* with their hair, that it was not attractive, and that the style needed to change. For many of the host mothers, braids were associated with Haitian women (although this idea changed over time as more students with braids came to the Dominican Republic from the United States).

Dominican American students also experienced similar "pressure" when host mothers mentioned the salon. Again, while some of the Dominican

American women students wore their hair in a straight style, others preferred to wear natural curly locks. Commenting that this is how they *liked their hair*, they resisted the social pressure to change it. To host mothers, students become the "host daughters," and since pre-teen and teenage girls often go to the salons with their mothers, this invitation by the host mothers could be interpreted as a nice gesture, but the students did not feel that way because of the politics of the salon. As Candelario (2000, 135) explains: "The Dominican salon acts as a socializing agent. Hair care and salon use are rites of passage into Dominican women's community. At the salon, girls and women learn to transform their bodies—through hair care, waxing, manicuring, pedicuring, facials, and so forth—into socially valued, culturally specific, and race-determining displays of femininity." These students valued their hair the way it was, and the braids, dreadlocks, short naturals, and curly locks meant something to them culturally; their hair was a personal reflection of *who they were* (Craig 2002; Rooks 1996). So, many of them took the invitation to the salon as an affront.

Over time, in the Dominican Republic, I was defined as *india clara, mulata*, and Dominican. African American students spent a shorter amount of time in the country but were still faced with new definitions of themselves because of the Dominican racial system. They often had to come to terms with being "mixed," defined as *indio* or *india*, Dominican and/or Haitian, and importantly for some of them, *not* being defined as black. For the students who were defined as black, this often meant that they were perceived to be Haitian. One of the students said during the one-month meeting, "I don't mind being thought of as Haitian because I do look like them. It's just that it is not who I am." The students who were considered black were viewed outside of the cultural and historical context of the United States, albeit within the context of the African diaspora. The situation was also difficult for many of the students who were not defined as black but rather as mixed. This was traumatic for many students who had a firm sense of themselves, their racial identities, and their history in the United States.

Importantly, the idea that self-defined black students from the United States could be divided due to Dominican notions of race, color, and ancestry was unsettling. On the one hand, darker-skinned African American students were still defined as black, being considered to be of Haitian, or perhaps of Jamaican descent, in the Dominican Republic. Lighter-skinned African American students, on the other hand, were defined as Dominican and/or *indio/a* (Simmons 2006). In the United States, they were part of the same community and were defined as black (perhaps light-skinned and dark-skinned according to colorization naming practices), but in the

Dominican Republic, they were viewed differently based on color, hair type and style, and other physical characteristics. The discussion here shows that both African Americans and Dominicans tried to make sense of their own identities and sense of history within a new context where they are defined in new ways. African Americans came to understand "mixedness" and Dominican blackness while Dominicans came to understand American blackness, creating an epistemological shift in both mixedness and blackness for both African Americans and Dominicans.

In sum, the idea of mixture is recast based on lived experiences both *here* and *there*. Socialization occurs within a particular context where ideas about race and color are often called into question as people encounter new racial systems, ideas of mixture, and categories that are both familiar and unfamiliar to them. It is in this vein that we *see* how identities are not only constructed but contested and later reconstructed. With *mulato* on the *cédula*, earlier notions of *mestizo* and *indio* are challenged and help to uncover the African past. The black amnesia, present for much of the twentieth century, is being reversed by people who are re-creating circumstances, and reconstructing history and identities. There is a conscious effort to remember.

Dominicans in the United States and the Question of Blackness

Haitians may be defined as black in the Dominican Republic, but in the United States Haitians are one group of many who are defined and define themselves as black. As a result, when Dominicans travel to the United States, they encounter other black referents, in particular African Americans. Ochy Curiel, the former director of Identidad de las Mujeres Afro in the Dominican Republic, encountered African American and other women in the United States and reflected on what it meant to be black, and more specifically *india*. Not only did she see women who looked like her, but they were also defining themselves and her in different ways. When she returned to the Dominican Republic, she began defining herself as Afro-Dominican in large part because of her experiences with and around African Americans, who considered her to be black. Edward's experience in Washington, D.C., where he was greeted by "what's up" with a nod of the head, as described earlier, is relevant here because of the positioning that took place to locate him as a "member" of the black community. Also, Edward and Ochy are what African Americans would consider to be light-skinned, and the fact that they were both defined as black in the United States offers another example of blackness moving away from the idea of dark skin color as was associated with Haiti and Haitians.

In New York in 2003, the play *Platanos and Collard Greens* was performed at the Producer's Club Theater. Based on the book *Do Platanos Go Wit Collard Greens* (Lamb 1994), the play focuses attention on relationships among the African American and Latino/a communities, images and representations of both groups, and race and gender. The social relationships that exist between African Americans and Dominicans are critical in understanding some of the shifts in identity that are taking place both in the United States and in the Dominican Republic. For Dominicans who attend a historically black college or university or pledge a predominantly African American fraternity or sorority, ideas of race and identity are called into question. This is not to say that culturally constructed ideas of *indio* will be completely abandoned, but it does suggest that new ideas of race may, and do, emerge.[4] There is reciprocity here in that African Americans are also influenced by Dominicans both here in the United States and when they travel to the Dominican Republic (Simmons 2006).

In 2004, Ginetta Candelario conducted an interview with Edwidge Danticat, Loida Maritza Pérez, Myriam J. A. Chancy, and Nelly Rosario—women writers from the island of Hispaniola—for the journal *Meridians: Feminism, Race, Transnationalism*. During the interview, Candelario asked the question, "So how does writing from outside the island affect your view of the island, its people, its realities, and its myths?" (2004, 75). Nelly Rosario responded in part: ". . . Having been raised here, I have the benefit of a movement around race in the United States, having been brought up with a black consciousness, which is something I can bring to the table, into my person, in my belief system. Maybe if I were on the island, I probably wouldn't. I'm not saying that there are not people who do have that consciousness and who are working within that, but just from how I grew up, my family, my origins, I don't think I could've made that big leap. Because again, it's the shame around color, the shame around race, and the shame around sexuality, too" (75).

Loida Maritza Pérez responded to the same question: "Those who remain have myths about their history, culture, class, and race as those who leave. The difference is that those who leave are more prone to question those myths. Think of it simply as perspective. Having stepped away, immigrants view things from a different angle and notice gaps and oversights, which prevents us from subscribing wholesale to those myths. Take, for example, the myth that Dominicans are *Indios*, or Spanish. These myths negate the African and purposefully warp history" (76).

Both Rosario and Pérez discuss Dominican identity and notions of race based on their experiences and critical reflections of race and identity in the

United States. Rosario suggests that being in the Dominican Republic may not have brought about the black consciousness she now experienced as a result of being in the United States. And as Pérez comments, one's perspective on race can change through immigration, and for her, her understanding of Dominican history has changed. Both of these women speak to issues that I would like to raise in this work—ideas about black consciousness, shame about color and race, and a "warped" sense of history that has negated the African past.

The next chapter maps the process of reconstructing Dominican racial identity along the lines of being Afro-Dominican, *negro/a*, and/or *mulato/a* in the Dominican Republic. Specifically, it examines how Dominican actors—scholars and activists—are actively working to assert and promote Afro-Dominicanness, and, as a result, are unburying the African past in the Dominican Republic.

Africanidad and Afro-Dominican

Alliances, Organizations, and Networks in the African Diaspora

"Y tu abuela, donde está?"
Poem by the Puerto Rican poet Fortunato Vizcarrondo in *Dinga y mandinga*

The tale of Dominican blackness contains the elements of a bad story, dominated by the theme of Negrophobia, and a good story, consisting of a narrative of events that show Santo Domingo setting the pattern of the struggle for freedom and racial equality in the Americas.
Silvio Torres-Saillant, "Blackness and Meaning
in Studying Hispaniola: A Review Essay"

... Llamamos amnesia negra, al esfuerzo que ha hecho la ideología dominante por minimizar o, cuando no, desconocer, la presencia de lo negro en nuestro país; no sólo en relación a los componentes de la cultura: música, religión, comida, danza, gestos, adornos, criterios estéticos, organización social, sino también en cuanto a los aspectos físico-raciales (We call it black amnesia, the effort that the dominant ideology has made to minimize, or refuse to acknowledge, the African presence in our country; not only in relation to the cultural components: music, religion, food, dance, gestures, adornments, aesthetics, social organization, but also with respect to the physical racial aspects).
Carlos Andújar, *Identidad Cultural y Religiosidad Popular*

Sherezada "Chiqui" Vicioso, an accomplished Dominican poet, migrated to the United States in the 1960s. Before that time, she considered herself to be *india clara*. However, this was called into question in the United States as she entered the country and settled into her neighborhood. She wrote about the experience in the journal *Callaloo*:

"Your passport . . ."
"Aquí está."
"What is this business of 'india clara'?"
"That is my color. In Santo Domingo we are classified by skin color. I am 'india clara,' that means 'light indian' . . ."
"Indian is not a color . . ."

"Look, I don't have time for that kind of business."

In fact no one seemed to have time to explain to me that kind of business that I had labored to accept by means of hair straighteners and Perlina's skin lightening cream; by the sheer force of listening that I had to marry a white man so that I could improve the "race" because by some terrible genetic mistake or some secret vengeance, my sister and I had turned out "indias claras" like our father who was not "indian" [sic] but "jabao," that is to say, sort of red, with kinky hair, and some freckles . . . But, there are no indians left in Santo Domingo! my indian friends from Central and South America would utter in disbelief . . .

Yes, but there we have been classified that way. I am light indian; if I were darker I would be called "india india" and if "I were hopeless," I would be known as "india canela," a "cinnamon colored indian" . . .

But it all got sort of complicated when we moved to a neighborhood in New York where there were "morenos" (black Americans) who looked like us girls. . . . (Vicioso 2000, 1014–15)

Chiqui's experience with race in the Dominican Republic—defining herself as *india clara*, straightening her hair, and using whitening or lightening cream—is common for many Dominican women. I first met Chiqui in 1998 at a poetry reading in Santiago and learned about her experience in the United States, in the 1960s, when she was influenced by the civil rights movement and African American women like Angela Davis. Perhaps it was because of the socio-historical moment of her migration to the United States, that over time Chiqui deconstructed *india clara* and reconstructed *mulata* and Afro-Dominican identities, aligning herself with other similarly positioned women in the United States and throughout the African diaspora. During the poetry reading, Chiqui recounted the story about her first experience at the airport, saying that it was one of the most profound experiences that she has had, and it became a defining moment for her because up until that point no one had ever challenged her racial identity. She was *india clara* in the Dominican Republic and was suddenly told that she could not be *india clara* in the United States. This was just the first of many challenges that Chiqui faced that would prompt her to call into question her identity and history.

Chiqui attended Brooklyn College and was surrounded by other Dominicans, other people from the Caribbean, and African Americans. As she put it, in this context, she came to realize that the rest of the world viewed the Dominican Republic as part of the Caribbean—but for her until this point, countries such as Jamaica, Puerto Rico, and Cuba were *part of the Caribbean.* Earlier in the book, I talked about the Dominican Republic being conceptualized as part of the West Indies; this changed during the Trujillo regime, when in an effort to link the Dominican Republic to Spain, references to the West Indies and the Caribbean were not as prevalent as before. Chiqui said that her experience in the United States taught her a lot about herself and how she viewed the Dominican Republic. In the United States, she started to be more critical in her thinking and reflected on how she was socialized. "I really hadn't thought about bleaching creams and the emphasis on 'marrying up' until I was in the United States."[1]

Chiqui was in the United States during the civil rights movement and was influenced by everything that was happening around her with regard to racial and gender discrimination. As she continued talking about her experiences, she said, "I was influenced by Angela Davis and the Black Panthers and wanted to be like Angela. I learned a lot from the black community in the U.S." When she signed my book after the poetry reading, she wrote, "Kimberly Simmons: Because I have learned so much from your country and your women. Thanks." She went on to say that because of her experience in the United States, she defined herself most often as *mulata* and stressed that the Dominican Republic was composed primarily of *mulatos* and *negros.* Her experience illustrates how identities come to be articulated in various contexts. Chiqui realized that how she chooses to self-identify, as *mulata,* may not be affirmed in the Dominican Republic because of her being defined "locally" as *india clara.* Thus, among other *mulato*-identified people, she is *mulata,* and among *india*-identified people, she is still *india.* Although she claims both identities, her socio-racial identity depends on which group she's with and how they define her—in other words, it is the context in which we find ourselves that facilitates the ways in which identities shift.

In 1998, dressed in West African attire, Chiqui gave a keynote address at the Afro-Latin American Research Association (ALARA) conference in Santo Domingo (fig. 4.1). Chiqui's address was in both Spanish and English, and she talked about her migration experience to the United States, including what prompted her to question *indio* and her own identity, culminating in a new consciousness about race and the Dominican Republic as part of the Caribbean. After thanking Blas Jiménez for inviting her to speak at the conference, she credited him by saying, "Blas is a pioneer in this type of work . . . what has been a folkloric attempt to recuperate our roots." She went on to say that Blas founded a center twenty years ago and that he was instrumental in the creation of a group known as Octubre Mulato (October Mulatto). Octubre Mulato focused on "what it was to be black, to be Afro

Figure 4.1. Chiqui Vicioso at the ALARA Conference, Santo Domingo, 1998. Photo by the author.

in terms of music, hair, physical attributes . . . but there wasn't a conscious-ness here about the Black movement [or about] what was happening in the United States, in the Caribbean, in all parts. . . ." The founding of Octubre Mulato is related to the idea behind Día de la Raza (Race Day)—an acknowl-edgment of Columbus Day—and commemorates the encounters between Europeans, Native Americans, and Africans that resulted in the "mixed" population later referred to as *mulato*.

Similar to what Chiqui wrote about in the passage quoted earlier, she talked about her earliest experience with race in the United States with a U.S. Customs official: "I migrated to the United States in 1967. . . . The first question I received in the United States going through Customs was about the business of *indio*. We lived in Queens, and my mother would call black Americans *morenos*. These things caught my attention but did not create a consciousness yet."

This consciousness was a result of several experiences, being a minority student (student of color) at Brooklyn College, and organizing a conference with a focus on the Caribbean: "In 1965, Lyndon B. Johnson created what was called a system of minority quotas. That's to say that if a university received federal funds it had to have a quota of blacks and Hispanics in order to receive the funds, and all of the universities that had been prejudiced and closed to minorities went out and recruited minorities so they could receive federal funds. What happened? A group of eight Dominicans entered Brooklyn College. What an extraordinary experience. We were not taken seriously at any level, meaning we were their token minorities that they had to have so they could have their federal funds. The treatment we got from the teachers was amazing."

Referring to the Civil Rights Act of 1964 and affirmative action and targeted recruitment strategies, Chiqui recalls how she and other Dominican students entered Brooklyn College. It was here that she soon realized that Dominicans and others were grouped together under a larger "black" umbrella: "Something else that was interesting for us Dominicans, like blacks, is that we were with blacks from Jamaica, Barbados, Trinidad, and the French Caribbean. For Dominicans, the Caribbean is Cuba and Puerto Rico; the English and French Caribbean don't exist, not even Haiti and it is next to us. My entrance to Brooklyn College was a way—a discovery. Regardless of what I thought of myself at that time, I was considered a black woman. Secondly, I was a Caribbean woman. It was an identity and a geographical issue. We formed the Third World People's Coalition. That was the only way I could survive at Brooklyn College."

Chiqui makes the point that it did not matter what she considered herself to be; she knew that she was considered to be a black woman and also a Caribbean woman, and she had never thought of herself in this way before. As she said, and this is a common sentiment in the Dominican Republic, the Caribbean refers to other countries, not the Dominican Republic, which is imagined to be a Latin American country. Her experience at Brooklyn College played a large role in her consciousness-raising process as she located herself and the Dominican Republic within the context of the Caribbean and the African diaspora.

As a result of their experience at Brooklyn College, Chiqui and other students formed the Third World People's Coalition: "The Third World People's Coalition provided a way to begin to learn about Caribbean theoreticians. We had our first conference and met C. L. R. James, and through him, we learned about Marcus Garvey, and we began to study Franz Fanon. It was then that I discovered a book that was fundamental for my political and personal formation. That book was the doctoral thesis of Eric Williams called *Capitalism and Slavery*. This was a reflection on my identity—emotional, intellectual, and physical—in the United States. I am talking to you all about a first immigration, a first diaspora, where I learned about Afro-Americans."

The conference provided a forum to explore and learn more about the Caribbean region, history, and culture. Some years later, Chiqui went to West Africa, to Guinea-Bissau as part of a team and learned more about Africa and its influence and contribution to the diaspora. All of these experiences, in sum, contributed to raising her own consciousness.

Emergence of Black and African-Derived References in Cable Television and Music

Images from the United States are accessible to viewers in the Dominican Republic through cable television and the internet. One American influence that easily can be seen is naming practices. The following example is taken from my field notes in 1998 after my family and I attended a birthday party for the one-year-old daughter of a friend:

> We went to Stella's christening this morning and returned from her birthday party this evening with Asha. There were about twenty adults and fifteen children in the apartment. I said that I would take pictures and videotape the party. It did not take long for the party to divide along gender lines, with the men sitting outside and the women in the kitchen preparing the snacks and sitting with the kids in the living room. I sat by a woman I did not know and began talking to her when her daughter came up and asked her if she could go outside. She responded, "You can go outside and sit with your father, Kenia." I was curious that her daughter was named Kenia because it is a common name in the African American community and wondered how she decided to name her daughter Kenia. When I asked her, she said, "I did not know what to name her, and I asked my husband. He was watching TV one day, a program from *allá* [the United States] and saw a woman whose name was Kenia—she looked like us, and we both liked the name." I told her that I too liked the name and that it was common in the United States and that "Kenia is a country in Africa" [Kenia is the Spanish spelling of Kenya]. At this point, she looked at me and said, "I did not know that." On our way home, I found out that David had had the exact same conversation with Kenia's father about her name, and the father said he did not know that Kenya was a country in Africa.

Shortly after the birthday party, I read in a newspaper that one of Sammy Sosa's daughter's is also named "Kenia." In recent years, there has been increased interaction between Dominicans and African Americans and other groups of African descent throughout the Americas, in part because of perceived similarities and racial awareness in the United States:

> When Dominicans come to the United States, however, they escape the ideological artillery that sustains negrophobic thought in the homeland, and they have a greater possibility of coming to terms with their real ethnicity. In North America, a racially segregated society where the color of one's skin has often mattered more than the content of one's character in obtaining jobs and opportunities, Dominicans may find it expedient to assert their blackness. Cognizant that the larger white society does not differentiate racially between them and Haitians or other dark-skinned Caribbeans, Dominicans become accustomed to speaking of themselves as a "people of color" and ally themselves with the other peoples of color in the struggle for survival. (Torres-Saillant and Hernández 1998, 143–44)

The above statement links Dominicans with a larger homogenization process of blackness in the United States. While there may be language, social class, and other differences, some of these features are flattened due to phenotype and whom Dominicans are perceived *to be*. Here, Torres-Saillant and Hernández hint at a larger black community that forms in the daily struggles for survival. Black ethnic groups also form as a result of the differences along the lines of nationality, language, and cultural practices (Waters 1999). Nonetheless, the United States is a place where Dominicans and Haitians have more in common than not and where distinctions that are made in the Dominican Republic are not made in the United States—the United States is also a place where connections are made with other peoples of African descent based on perceived similarities in experience and history. Also, as in Chiqui's experience, Dominicans, like other black ethnic groups, were able to take advantage of some of the federal funding to increase diversity.

Again, one of the differences, at present, in the United States is the lack of an in-between racial category that defines people of mixed African and European descent. As discussed earlier, color categories exist within the African American community that are similar to *indio* (that is, light-skinned and dark-skinned), but there are no official mixed categories at present ("mixed" is an informal term that captures the sense of mixture). In a larger "black" social space, there is room for exchange and increased interactions between groups. Such interactions and exposure through media have a mutual influencing effect on socio-racial categories as discussed above as well as on naming practices, hairstyles (that is, twists and curly locks), music (for example, merengue hip-hop and merengue house, Latin jazz, and so forth): "... Proyecto Uno has succeeded in creating an aesthetic of its own by drawing from Dominican and Latin sounds and mixing them with elements of rap, house, and other musical modalities from hip-hop urban culture in the United States" (Torres-Saillant and Hernández 1998, 138).

Merengue house and merengue hip-hop are very popular musical forms, and Proyecto Uno is one of the more popular groups with crossover appeal with Spanish lyrics mixed with English. Fulanito (a group composed of Dominican Americans) is another popular group with mass appeal. Some of their songs are recorded entirely in English and played on radio stations and clubs in the United States. Using *negro* and *mulato* in songs has been a practice for a long time. References to *mulata* and *negra* often carry a sexual overtone with sexualized imagery. For example, Fulanito's song "5 Mira" on its *Popular Songs* album describes the way a *negra* moves to the music in such a way that you'd want to get next to her:

mira como mueve esa negra chula
mira como mueve esa negra chula
con su cinturita que sabrosura
con su cinturita que sabrosura

mira negra chula
mira que sabrosura
mira
mira
hecha pa aca mi morenita te quiero apretar

look how that "cool" *negra* moves
look how that "cool" *negra* moves
with her little tempting waist
with her little tempting waist

look "cool" *negra*
look tempting *negra*
look
look
come close, my *morenita*, I want to be close to you [your body].

Here, there is attention to how the *negra* dances in a very tempting way to the onlookers, provoking a sexual response. This is just one example of *negra*, *morena*, and *mulata* in Dominican music.

Recent years have not only witnessed the emergence of merengue hip-hop and merengue house but also a shift in merengue, *bachata*, salsa, reg-gaeton, and R&B music. Salsa, once only understood by Spanish-speakers, is now recorded by some artists in English; Mark Anthony and India have songs in English. The rap artist 50 Cent remade one of his songs, "In da Club," into a merengue song heard in the Dominican Republic. I heard it for the first time when I was attending a birthday party in Santiago; it is a fast remix of the original song. It soon became one of my favorite songs, one I often requested at parties. And recently, Karina Pasian, the daughter of Dominican immigrants, performed at the White House at a celebration of black music for then President and Mrs. Bush. Karina's musical style in the R&B tradition has been compared to Alisha Keyes. Her debut album *First Love*, was released in August 2008. She is also the goddaughter of the famed composer Quincy Jones.

Merengue music is growing in popularity throughout the United States in salsa clubs and via Latin aerobics like Zumba, while documentaries like *Mad Hot Ballroom* introduce merengue music to people in the United States who might not otherwise be familiar with it. The actress Judy Reyes, who plays the role of Carla Espinosa on the television show *Scrubs*, often comments on being Dominican and not Puerto Rican on the show. Her character is married to an African American, Chris Turk, played by Donald Faison. Intermarriage between Dominicans and African Americans is common. One of the first examples I saw of "Afro-Dominican" was in *Ebony* maga-zine. Benjamin Chavis, the executive director of the NAACP in 1993 and 1994, appeared with wife, Martha, and their children, and the caption read that she was from the Dominican Republic and that *he* defined her as Afro-Dominican. What is not clear, however, is whether she defines herself this way (see fig. 4.2).

Africanidad and the Emergence of Afro-Dominican Identity

I use the term *africanidad* to talk about the discourse of linking people on a macro-level across borders and nationalities in the African diaspora. *Mu-lataje* and *africanidad* are fairly new discourses surrounding race and nation and the articulation of new identities based on experiences outside of the Dominican Republic, a critical reading of history, and reflection on the past. *Africanidad* is less concerned with an intermediate category and defining mixture and is more concerned with the reclaiming of an African ancestry and linking the Dominican nation with an African past.

During a brief stop at home, Chavis spends time with his wife, Martha, a native of the Dominican Republic whom he describes as an "Afro-Dominican," son Franklin, 3, and daughter Ana, 2.

Figure 4.2. Ben and Martha Chavis and family, *Ebony*, July 1993. Courtesy of *Ebony*.

Africanidad and *mulataje* overlap in the sense that they both recognize African ancestry and emerge as a result of experiences outside of the Dominican Republic that cause periods of reflection. However, while *mulataje* is linked to the *mulato* race/color category, *africanidad* asserts a *negro* and/or *afro-dominicano* (Afro-Dominican) identity. The main difference between the two discourses is that *mulataje* still captures a sense of racial "inbetweenness," and *africanidad* extends beyond mixture per se to address issues of ancestry and similarities throughout the African diaspora. *Mulato* is also more widespread in its use in the Dominican Republic than Afro-Dominican, an idea that will be discussed further at the end of this chapter.

Africanidad refers to the African diaspora and organizations that are making claims about being black and/or Afro-Dominican, linking themselves and their experiences in the Americas with African Americans and others in the diaspora (for example, Torres-Saillant 1995; Minority Rights Group 1995). *Africanidad* reclaims African ancestry and involves organizing efforts with other peoples of African descent to articulate a new discourse of race and nation—one that springs forth due to increased transnational migration and personal and group reflections on history. This was the case with the Casa por la Identidad de las Mujeres Afro (House for the Identity of the African-Descended Women) known as Identidad.

La Casa por la Identidad de las Mujeres Afro (Identidad)

Identidad was founded in 1989 by a group of self-defined black Dominican women who also defined themselves as being feminists (Simmons 2001). At present, as a result of the lack of funding, the organization is no longer functioning as such, but the work continues by the women who are dedicated to the goals established at the time of its founding. In the 1990s, Identidad was composed of approximately twenty core members and was located in the capital of Santo Domingo. While the leadership was composed of women with a college education, the general membership was quite diverse. Most of the women resided in urban areas and were involved with other organizations for women's economic and social betterment. Identidad was determined to reach women across social class lines.

While most of the members resided in the capital, others lived in Santiago, as well as in other parts of the Dominican Republic. They held occasional meetings, traveled to conferences, went to the United States to work or visit family, conducted research, and facilitated workshops. These workshops provided a forum for what they termed a "period of reflection" and were discussions of race-, color-, and gender-related topics. Members in Santo Domingo frequently traveled to Santiago and other cities in order to bring these ideas to women outside the capital. By facilitating workshops with women throughout the country, Identidad reached out and raised awareness across social class lines to the extent that claiming a black identity, and later an "Afro-Dominican identity," extended beyond women in the middle class.

In 1993, I left copies of *Essence* magazine with Identidad (members had requested African American women's magazines, and I had some with me). At the time, I did not realize the impact this popular black women's magazine would have on the organization with regard to image. When I returned in 1995 to continue research, Identidad was using the image of Susan L. Taylor, the former editor-in-chief of *Essence*, on the cover of its newsletter, *Red de Mujeres Afrocaribeñas y Afrolatinoamericanas* (Network of Afro-Caribbean and Afro-Latin American Women).[2] The director of Identidad, at that time explained that Taylor and her corn-rowed hair image represented their ideal of beauty and strength (see fig. 4.3).

Identidad identified five organizational objectives: 1) to promote a broad process of reflection that serves as a premise in the search of identity; 2) to help other women become aware of the relationship between racial and gender discrimination and oppression; 3) to reveal the contributions of the black woman in the formation of the nation; 4) to demythologize the domi-

Boletina Informativa

Año I • N° 5 • Diciembre 1994   *Santo Domingo, República Dominicana*

Red de Mujeres

Afrocaribeñas
y
Afrolatinoamericanas

Figure 4.3. Identidad newsletter featuring Susan Taylor from *Essence*. Courtesy of Identidad.

nant stereotypes about the black woman; and 5) to convey ideas that advance accurate models of identity with regard to the black woman.[3]

Later, during this same year, a rupture occurred within the organization over its name and the terminology used to describe women's experiences within the group. Identidad's original name was Identidad de la Mujer Negra (Identity of the Black Woman). This became problematic. In particular, a small contingent of lighter-complexioned women questioned the exactness and accuracy of the term *negra* in the organization's name to capture their experiences, *negra* being a term usually reserved for Haitians, Africans, and extremely dark-complexioned Dominicans. The label "black"—

with its contentious historical and contemporary meanings—became the focal point of what amounted to a protracted exercise in identity politics. Other phenotypic traits also came into question, namely hair and the way it was styled—rejecting the use of hair relaxers and straighteners and instead wearing hair "natural" (for example, afros, braids, curly locks, and so forth). Color, as a distinguishing feature, was also interrogated by the women as light-skinned women were made to feel that they were not "black enough." Light-skinned Dominican women in Identidad, while they defined themselves as black, were, at times, met with looks of disapproval or confusion by darker-skinned women in the organization. This is something that also happens in the United States among African Americans in social organizations around issues of authenticity.

The end result of this rupture was the founding of Cafe con Leche (Coffee with Milk), a new, albeit short-lived, organization that articulated new notions of race, mixture, color, and gender in the Dominican Republic. Identidad did not have a large membership, so when Cafe con Leche formed with some of the original members of Identidad, it had an impact on the organization not only in terms of members but also in terms of focus. In effect the coexistence of Identidad and Cafe con Leche divided these Dominican feminists into *negra* and *mulata* camps. In response to this newly formed and competing organization, Identidad underwent reorganization and redefinition after what was termed another period of reflection and renamed itself by replacing *negra* with *afro* (as in *afro-dominicana*). The purpose was to re-create Identidad and reunite the group by bringing women from Cafe con Leche back into Identidad—which is what happened. One of the founding members of Identidad, and former member of Cafe con Leche, Ochy Curiel, became the new director of Identidad (fig. 4.4).

As demonstrated here, by moving away from black as a *color* marker as well as a *racial* one, women redefined themselves as Afro-Dominican, focusing on African heritage, recognizing the African diasporic experience with regard to mixture, and linking themselves with other women of African descent in the Americas and throughout the diaspora. Ochy commented that "they began to question the significance of black as a descriptive category and decided, after a period of reflection, that they were of African descent, with mixture, and it was important to claim an Afro-Dominican identity, which includes all *mulata* and *black* Dominican women."[4]

Identidad worked to raise awareness about racism and sexism, making claims that race and gender, along with class and sexuality, need to be focal points in research and articulations of Dominicanness. Part of this meant that the group aligned itself with Haitian women and other women of the African diaspora as a response to the marginalization they experience in the

Figure 4.4. Ochy Curiel, the director of Identidad de las Mujeres Afro, and Kimberly Eison Simmons. Photo by David S. Simmons.

Dominican Republic—expressing their identity as Afro-Dominican. The use of Afro- as a way of reclaiming and embracing African ancestry is radical in the Dominican Republic, because while ideas of mixture persist, they are not typically explained with reference to blacks as many Dominicans maintain distance from both blackness and having an African ancestry and past (see fig. 4.3).

Since its inception in 1989, Identidad has hosted the first meeting of Black Latin American and Caribbean Women in the summer of 1992. In 1993, it also participated in the Cross-Cultural Black Women's Studies Summer Institute in Venezuela. It held a feminist workshop that I attended in Santiago in May 1998 where it discussed plans for an upcoming meeting of Latin American and Caribbean feminists in 1999. The group also sponsored a workshop on combating racism in 1998. Along with the new reorganization from *negra* to *afro* came a new mission and revised objectives:

Es una organización de mujeres de origen afro que enmarcamos nuestro trabajo en la transformación de las estructuras sociales y políticas reproductoras y transmisoras de ideologías que fomentan los prejuicios raciales y por condición de género. . . . La misión de Identidad es enfrentar todo tipo de discriminación étnico racial, rescatar y promover los aportes de la cultura afro a nuestra conformación social. Los lineamientos estrategicos parten de: a) empoderar a las mujeres negras en el rescate de su identidad afro a traves de lo simbólico, lo artistico, y lo religioso; b) la denuncia de todo tipo de discriminación a cualquier persona por su condición étnico racial o de género; c) la investigación; d) la articulación para combatir el racismo y el sexismo. . . .[5]

(It is an organization of women of African origin that frames our work in the transformation of the social structures and political reproducers and transmitters of ideologies that evoke the racial prejudices and for the condition of gender. . . . The mission of Identidad is to confront all types of racial/ethnic discrimination, to rescue and promote the contributions of the African culture to our social fabric. The strategic boundaries consist of: a) empowering those black women in the rescue of their Afro-identity through the symbolic, the artistic, and the religious; b) denouncing all types of discrimination of any person based on their racial/ethnic status or gender; c) research; d) the articulation to combat racism and sexism. . . .)

The above objectives highlight the point that it is necessary to "rescue" or recover Afro-Dominican identity as this has been buried in the historical memory. The group linked its recovery with a mission to combat sexism and racism while combining research and action.

Its mission was further articulated in a public forum organized by the group at the public library in Santo Domingo in July 1998. During the course of the discussion, entitled "Que Somos Etnicamente las Dominicanas y los Dominicanos" (What We Dominicans Are Ethnically), which I attended, Ochy explained why Identidad is advancing an Afro-Dominican identity:

. . . Yo pienso que hay una identidad más global que es la caribeña, y yo pienso que ciertamente independiente de las diferencias que podamos tener y ahora que estamos haciendo estudios sobre eso, no podemos pensar en el Caribe como una unidad porque inclusive dentro del Caribe hay una diversidad increíble. El Caribe es ya una construcción histórica que hemos ido creando a través de los años y que es parte de nuestra identidad, aunque no la asumimos, a pesar es desde esa óptica que se nos ve desde fuera. Qué sucede aquí en este pedazo de isla?

Cómo definirla étnicamente, sea un proceso de construcción, sea una cuestión de que estratégicamente sea más válido asumir certa categoría u otra? Yo me inclino evidentemente por la propuesta Afro-Dominicana en el sentido de que para mi, y yo no soy una estudiosa del tema, sino que es una opción más sentimental y militante que otra cosa, la propuesta de la categoría Afro-Dominicana me resuelve la mezcla, es decir lo dominicano es una construcción histórica de mezclas de culturas: hispana, africana e indígena—aunque por opción política optamos por destacar aun que otra o eliminar una y otra. Ahora bien yo creo que hay un predominio de la cultura africana que se ha adaptado a los tiempos. Aquí, y hay evidencias, el elemento afro es fundamental—por eso Identidad de las Mujeres Afro.

(I think that there is an identity more global that is the Caribbean, and I think that certainly independent of the differences that we can have and now that we are conducting research on that, we cannot think of the Caribbean like a unit because inside the Caribbean there is incredible diversity. The Caribbean is already a historical construction that we have created through the years and is part of our identity, although we don't assume it, and it is from that lens that we are seen/viewed from the outside. What happens here on this piece of island?

How to define someone ethnically, a process of construction, a question of what category is more strategically valid to assume? I am inclined to lean toward the proposal *afro-dominicana* in the sense that for me, and I am not an expert on the topic, but rather it is a sentimental and militant option more than anything else; the proposal of the category *afro-dominicana* resolves for me the mixture, that is to say that Dominican is a historical construction of mixtures of cultures: Spanish, African, and indigenous—although for political preference we opt to highlight one over another. Now, I believe that there is a predominance of the African culture that has adapted over time. Here, and there are evidences, the African element is fundamental—for that reason Identidad of the African-Descended Women.)

Ochy suggests that there is tremendous diversity within the Caribbean and that it has been historically constructed—in a homogenizing way that flattens differences. She and Chiqui say that a "Caribbean" identity is one that Dominicans do not typically assume. For Ochy, Dominican identity calls for militancy and rescue of the African past in the articulation of mixture with a reference to Africa. While not designed to describe the mixture, the term Afro-Dominican takes into account the processes of mixture stemming from slavery and the colonial (and postcolonial) era. "Opting" to highlight one ancestry over another for "political reasons" is similar to being black in the United States (and the one-drop rule where African ancestry is highlighted). Also, Ochy recognized that the historical adoption and institutionalization of *indio* erased the African past and ancestral ties and also kept dark Dominicans on the dark side of the *indio* continuum.

Enrique, a Dominican scholar who lived in the United States and Canada, commented:

> No se puede hablar de la identidad sin tener en cuenta la cultural. Que es lo que diferencia una cultura de la otra, es precisamente la significación que nosotros tenemos sobre la vida, la muerte, relación hombre-mujer, la enfermedad. Eso es lo que diferencia una cultura de otra. . . . Si nosotros ponemos por ejemplo el caso de la gente que construye su identidad en un contexto multicultural, el caso de los dominicanos y dominicanas en los Estados Unidos, ellos y ellas tienen que lidiar con dos sistemas culturales distintos. . . . Otro aspecto que ha resurgido muy ligado a lo primero es el carácter dinámico de la identidad o sea la identidad no es una constante, no es una cosa pegada sobre la pared, es por el contrario es unidad de continuidad y cambio—el mismo ejemplo de los dominicanos en Nueva York nos sirve. Nosotros llegamos a los Estados Unidos con una identidad, con una idea de lo que somos, y cuando llegamos a los Estados Unidos de América, yo que nunca me he definido ni sentido negro—de repente yo aprendo por primera vez que soy negro y aquí yo soy un indio, entonces el individuo tiene que lidiar con todas estas asignaciones, con patrones con modelos diferentes y coger y dejar.

> (One cannot speak of the identity without keeping culture in mind. What is different from one culture to another is precisely the significance that we have about life, death, the relationship between man and woman, illness. That is what differentiates one culture from another. If we use the case that people construct their identity in a multicultural context, for example the case of Dominican men and women in the United States, they have to struggle against two different cultural systems. Another aspect that has reappeared is the dynamic character of identity, that is to say that identity is not a constant, it is not something stuck on a wall; on the contrary it is unit of continuity and change— the same example of the Dominicans in New York serves. We arrive in the United States with an identity, with an idea of what we are, and when we arrive in the United States of America, I had never defined myself or felt black—suddenly I learn for the first time that I am black and here [the Dominican Republic] I am an *indio*, then the individual

has to struggle with these appointments/naming, with standards with different models to grasp and to allow.)

Here, Enrique used a personal experience to illustrate what happens when two racial systems collide—it is the struggle to define who one *is* while being defined by others in a different place. The reconfiguration of identities is located in this site of struggle and negotiation. He suggests that Dominicans arrive with a sense of who they are and that "sense" changes in the United States because they are defined as black. On an individual level, it is a struggle of sorts, but on a much larger level, these same actors interact with both racial systems, and indirectly, and perhaps directly, play a part in transforming the racial system in the Dominican Republic. This is an example of ideas that come to reshape categories and definitions in the relocalization process.

Again, unlike *mulataje, africanidad* is less concerned about asserting an "in-between" racial category that "makes sense" across borders. Instead, it views Africa as an ancestral place that links the Dominican Republic to other places and Dominicans to other peoples of African descent. Therefore, groups organize around such objectives as combating racism, asserting identities, raising awareness, revising history, and aligning themselves by traveling to attend meetings around these issues.

By way of example, the poster that Identidad used in 1992, when it hosted the first international conference of Afro-Caribbean and Afro-Latin American women, in Santo Domingo, was used on the cover of a book entitled *Connecting Across Cultures and Continents: Black Women Speak Out on Identity, Race, and Development* (Pala 1995). The book contains papers that were given at the Fifth International Interdisciplinary Congress on Women in Costa Rica in 1993. Sergia Galvan, a member of Identidad, participated in the meeting in Costa Rica and discussed the relationship between race and gender oppression in Latin America:[6] "The economic and structural adjustment policies in most of the countries in Latin America, instead of supporting participation of Black women in the labour market, actually increase their poverty, marginalization and exploitation. Black women are found in the worst-paid jobs in housework and agriculture, and continue to be among the poorest in society" (Galvan 1995, 50).

It is often the case that race, as a factor in shaping women's lives in the Dominican Republic, is often ignored in favor of a social class analysis. Is it simply a coincidence that those who occupy the lowest rung of the socioeconomic ladder "happen" to be dark-skinned? Identidad was concerned with this question as it relates to Dominican women at home and abroad. One of the ways in which Dominican women are racialized abroad is through the traffic of women as commercial sex workers in Europe: "At the regional level, the traffic of women (and girls) is increasing dramatically day by day, especially of Black women. The myths and prejudices surrounding Black women's sexuality are used to promote and support the trafficking of Black females in order to satisfy men's sexual fantasies" (Galvan 1995, 50).

The traffic of women is a major concern in the Dominican Republic, especially among black feminists. Identidad was among one of the women's groups that helped educate Dominican women about other Dominican women who have been lured away under the premise that they would perform in Europe (singing, dancing); after their arrival, they realized that they were sought after for sex work. At the time that Identidad worked to bring about more awareness on this topic, allegedly half of the sex workers in the Netherlands were composed of Dominican women. Over the years, sexual tourism has become more racialized as German and other European men request the companionship of "black" women when they visit the Dominican Republic (Brennan 2004; Gregory 2006). Not only do European and American men fantasize about *morena* women in the Dominican Republic, but Dominican men also talk about women in racialized terms. In the summer of 2007 as I sat with David and friends in a park in Santo Domingo, I overheard a Dominican man say, "Quiero una morena. Voy a comprarme una morena" (I want a *morena*. I'm going to buy a *morena*).

Identidad has also organized around Columbus Day—locally referred to as Día de la Raza (Race Day)—in reference to the indigenous, European, and African "encounters." In recent years, various individuals and groups attended celebrations or presentations (at the PUCMM and elsewhere) to talk about Columbus and the legacy of the resultant encounters. The following commentary is taken from Identidad's newsletter and discusses the significance of Columbus Day:[7]

> En octubre se conmemora una feche importante para las y los latino-americanas/os y caribeñas/os. Para los sectores tradicionales y conservadores de nuestros países en la fecha del 12 de octubre constituye la celebración del día de la raza, el encuentro de culturas, para otros sectores octubre nos recuerda la masacre, la explotación de que fueron objeto grandes poblaciones indígenas y negras esclavas traídas desde el África como fuerza de trabajo para la acumulación de riquezas de la colonia española en el proceso de la mundialización del capitalismo.
>
> Fruto de este proceso de colonización que se ha impuesto hace hoy

506 años, la identidad de nuestros pueblos se presenta confusa, con tendencias a asumirnos solo como una parte de lo que somos, resaltando únicamente la herencia histórica de la cultura española, no así de la indígena y africana, lo que se nos revela en la cotidianidad en manifestaciones racistas que van desde las formas más sutiles ("en mi casa negro el caldero") hasta las más complejas ("se busca joven de buena presencia"). Octubre debe servir para seguir profundizando sobre el tema de la identidad y el racismo, recordando nuestro pasado histórico para poder construir un presente sin confusiones.

(In October an important date is commemorated for Latin Americans and Caribbeans. For the traditional and conservative sectors of our countries, October 12 constitutes the celebration of Race Day, the encounter of cultures, but in October other sectors remember the massacre, the exploitation of large populations of indigenous and black slaves brought from Africa as a work force for the accumulation of wealth of the Spanish colony in the process of world capitalism.

Because of this colonization process that began 506 years ago, the identity of our communities is confused, with tendencies to assume only a part of what we are, only referring to the historical inheritance of the Spanish culture, not the indigenous and African, which is revealed to us daily in the racist manifestations that go from the more subtle forms [in my house the pot is black] to the most complex [looking for a young person of good presence]. October should serve to continue intellectualizing about the topic of identity and racism, remembering our historic past in order to be able to construct a present without confusions.)

Here, *Cimarrona*, the name of Identidad's newsletter, is as revealing as what it discusses about Race Day. *Cimarrona* literally means "runaway slave woman" and not only brings attention to a "forgotten" slave society in the Dominican Republic but also a form of resistance used by the slaves themselves. Also of note is that there is a picture of a young girl with braids and beads in her hair—again, going against the social grain of what is acceptable (fig. 4.5). The women of Identidad continue in the spirit of resistance in their newsletter. For Identidad, Race Day represents the encounter of cultures and exploitation of indigenous and enslaved Africans in the process of world capitalism. The newsletter editorial suggests that there is a national confusion about "who they are," which is made evident by the constant reference to Spanish origins. Identidad, along with other groups and individuals

Octubre 1998

Año 2, No. 7

El porvenir también tiene que ser negro

sin racismo
sin sexismo
sin violencia

OCTUBRE

Un mes para recordar los efectos de la colonización

En octubre se conmemora una fecha importante para las y los latinoameri-canas/os y caribeñas/os. Para los sectores tradicionales y conservadores de nuestros países la fecha del 12 de octubre constituye la celebración del día de la raza, el encuentro de culturas, para otros sectores Octubre nos recuerda la masacre, la explotación de que fueron objeto grandes poblaciones indígenas y negras esclavas traídas desde el Africa como fuerza de trabajo para la acumulación de riquezas de la colonia española en el proceso de la mundialización del capitalismo.

Fruto de este proceso de colonización que se ha impuesto hace hoy 506 años, la identidad de nuestros pueblos se presenta confusa, con tenden-cias a asumirnos solo como una parte de lo que somos, resaltando únicamente la herencia histórica de la cultura española, no así de la indígena y africana, lo que se nos revela en la cotidianidad en manifesta-ciones racistas que van desde las formas más sutiles ("en mi casa negro el caldero") hasta las más complejas ("se busca joven de buena presencia ")

Octubre debe servir para seguir profundizando sobre el tema de la identidad y el racismo, recordando nuestro pasado histórico para poder construir un presente sin confusiones.

Figure 4.5. Identidad newsletter. Courtesy of Identidad.

writing newspaper essays and making television appearances on Race Day, claims that this day should be a day for reflection and consciousness striving to create a socio-historically accurate identity "without confusions."

Combining research and activism, women in Identidad conducted research and traveled to local, regional, and international meetings and conferences that focused on racial oppression of women in order to form alliances with other black women and to make their plight visible in the Dominican Republic. From the trafficking of women to sexual tourism on the island, from the prevalence of violence in the factories of the free trade zones to the role of women as mothers, as primary socializing agents of children (Safa 1995), Identidad rallied around a number of issues while promoting an "Afro" identity. Through its efforts, and along with other women's groups, Identidad has been able to bring about change in the Dominican Republic. And as the members of Identidad individually continue to make connections with other black women, recognizing the similarities and differences in terms of their experiences, they play a part in the reconfiguration of racial identities, and the redefinition of the Dominican Republic as part of the African diaspora.

Tourism, Representation, and Blackness

The Amber Museum in Puerto Plata showcases some of the finest amber in the country as well as fine wood carvings of Taíno-like figures. Haitians are known more for their wood carvings as this is associated with "African art." I asked one of the clerks if there was a Dominican artist working with the carvings, why they were using "indigenous" figures, and why they had carvings alongside the amber, and he responded by saying "No. They are Haitian artists, although some of them are working with Dominicans to show them how to do the carvings. The Taínos were the first people here—they were indigenous like the amber—so we have their images here in the museum. Tourists are really interested in the carvings—that is what they want." Thus, in addition to their labor in the sugar cane fields and construction projects throughout the Dominican Republic, Haitians are now being sought for their cultural production. Because of tourists' interest in carvings, Haitian artists are asked to create "Dominican" images and produce something "indigenous" utilizing their skills and tradition of woodcarving.

Something interesting emerges where tourism and guests' expectations intersect. On a family weekend trip to Puerto Plata, I had the opportunity to talk to some of the hotel workers about their experiences with Dominican and international tourists. The entertainment manager told me that she coordinates all of the evening shows as a result of assessing the interests of European and American guests. What often happened was that the shows used racialized images from the United States to create musical and comedy routines. We attended a variety show one evening during this particular stay. Many of the staff members that we had been interacting with during the day were performing in the show in the evening. Some of the acts were impersonations of artists such as Michael Jackson and Whitney Houston, but the one that was of particular interest to me was done in blackface with stereotypical images and slurred speech. The predominantly white audience laughed and clapped during the blackface performance. I wondered if the shock we felt was shared by anyone else. Then I wondered if the same racial attachments and the cultural and historical significance, with roots in the United States years, were linked to these images in a similar way that would be considered racist and stereotypical in the Dominican Republic (although I had seen a similar character in blackface on Dominican television on a mid-day program). I wondered how the audience interpreted the show—what *was* its significance in the Dominican Republic? Was this an "import" from the United States without the racial connotations? It is difficult to know, but I suspect that on the one hand, the performance could have been viewed as an American comedy form, thus stripped of its socio-historical racial overtones, but on the other hand, it could have been performed at the request of guests who wanted a certain "type" of show.

This reminds me of what Wright (1990) expressed about Afro-Venezuelans often being reminded of their "status" with negative images in cartoons despite the fact that race is not recorded on the Venezuelan census. Afro-Venezuelans were reminded of their slave history, and despite having money and education they still were descendants of slaves. The Dominican Republic does not have this particular legacy of "memory." Dominicans are not typically reminded that they are descendants of slaves—they are reminded that Haitians are descendants of slaves. And while there are racialized images of dark Dominican women as "mammy" and domestic figures associated with certain brands of foods (like Aunt Jemima in the United States), some of the other racialized and stereotypical images that might have been used in the United States or Venezuela were used to represent Haitians in the Dominican Republic, not Dominicans. This is changing, however.

Thus, the articulation of *africanidad* changes this perspective on Haiti, and on being of African descent. The linkage is one that connects people of African descent due to a sense of shared history, circumstance, and experience. The assertion of black or "Afro" identities then links Dominicans with Haitians, African Americans, Afro-Venezuelans, Puerto Ricans, and so forth. It is a stance that recasts history and the formation of the Dominican nation along the lines of a global black diasporic experience.

A Move to Unbury the African Past

RUTA DEL ESCLAVO (SLAVE ROUTE): UNESCO-SPONSORED SEMINAR

In March 2004 in Santo Domingo, UNESCO sponsored an international interdisciplinary seminar on the trans-Atlantic African slave trade and its consequences. I participated in the seminar and had the opportunity to meet other researchers and scholars from the Dominican Republic, other areas of the Caribbean, and the United States to discuss issues surrounding the slave trade and its impact. The poster for the event depicts the face of a man—possibly that of an enslaved African (fig. 4.6). It is significant that an international seminar entitled "The Slave Route" would be hosted in Santo Domingo—what has been referred to as the cradle of blackness in the Americas (Torres-Saillant 2000).

Figure 4.6. Poster from the Slave Route Seminar, Santo Domingo, 2004. Courtesy of the Comisión Nacional Dominicana de la Ruta del Esclavo.

E. LEÓN JIMENES CULTURAL CENTER

As discussed in the introduction, the E. León Jimenes Cultural Center or Centro León (http://www.centroleon.org.do), a privately funded cultural center in Santiago, is dedicated to the history and culture of the Dominican Republic. There are three interrelated exhibits in one of the wings of the cultural center representing Dominican heritage and ancestry. The Taíno exhibit re-creates scenes of how the Taínos lived and died as well as replicas of artifacts. The Spanish exhibit contains photos and documents as well as references to the Catholic Church and language. The African exhibit, at first glance, looks like a wall with rectangular pieces cut out. It's not until you approach the wall and look inside one of the openings that you see the most interesting part of this exhibit. Inside the enclosed wall are drums, food-stuffs, photos, bright colors, cloth, and references to music and dance. When I asked the guide about it, she said that unlike the indigenous and Spanish exhibits, the African exhibit represents how a great deal of the African past has been viewed—with a particular distance, obstruction, and as something you only see when you look close enough. In other words, the Africans, their presence, and their contribution have been buried. In many ways, the exhibit reflects the popular expression—we are all black "atrás de la oreja" (behind the ear)—blackness is hidden from sight.

A shift toward *mulataje* and *mulato* points to a new consciousness surrounding race and the ideas of being mixed with implied African ancestry. In sum, Identidad, Ruta del Esclavo, and the E. León Jimenes Cultural Center represent change and an attempt to uncover the African past and situate it within the context of the African diaspora while pointing to *afro-dominican-idad*. What we see is that Dominican racial identity is being reconstructed by the concerted efforts of scholars and activists as they challenge and promote categories and target socialization efforts to include the African past in textbooks, claim Afro-Dominicanness, and promote it throughout Dominican society.

Conclusion

Unburying the African Past

The African Diaspora

I began the book by questioning the issue of black denial in the Dominican Republic and asking if Dominicans were denying that they were black (as is often the assertion) or if their blackness had been denied by the state. I suggest that it is the latter. The African past was buried in textbooks, identity construction, and in the memory of Dominicans over time. European and Taíno ancestries were privileged and accentuated until very recently. Blas Jiménez, Chiqui Vicioso, Ochy Curiel and members of Identidad, and others serve as identity entrepreneurs working to unbury the African past, uncover the roots, and reconstruct and assert new identities.

These identity entrepreneurs worked against the backdrop of a national project that sought to define the majority of the population as mixed, *mestizo*, and *indio* as, over the years, Dominican peoplehood was defined with waves of immigration to the Dominican Republic. A new consciousness emerged as some Dominicans deconstructed their own history and sense of themselves often in relation to others who physically resembled them in the United States, throughout Latin America and the Caribbean, and the African diaspora.[1] Interactions with African Americans and the U.S. racial system is just one way that Dominican notions of race have been called into question. Importantly, this does not suggest that the United States "has it right" with regard to race and racial definitions, but the racial system of the United States reflects a worldview of blackness and whiteness that visitors and immigrants to the United States encounter. In fact, many Dominicans point to the experience in the United States, and being considered black in particular, as part of their own consciousness-raising process. Members of Identidad critically reflected on their experiences outside of the Dominican Republic with other people of African descent and formed a community of consciousness in the Dominican Republic. Afro-, black-, and mulatto-identified Dominicans are not only unburying the African past and roots but also asserting new identities and forming alliances with other similarly positioned people throughout the African diaspora.

Early in the book, I talked about the nation emerging as an important concern in the twentieth century due to the massive movement of people and ideas across borders, linking people in the formation of race and nation while co-constructing racial and national identities. This is the process where nationness is defined over time and space, and in this case, this process shaped changing ideas of Dominicanness. When people and ideas cross borders, they not only have an impact in the place of destination, but also in the place of origin as we see in the Dominican Republic. As Dominicans interacted with competing racial systems, within these different national contexts, they not only changed how they defined themselves, but they also had an impact on social structures in the Dominican Republic.

The Dominican Republic witnessed a large exodus of people in the post-Trujillo era due to economic restructuring policies that prompted more people to look to the United States as a place for economic and social advancement (Torres-Saillant and Hernández 1998). Over time, when Dominicans traveled between the Dominican Republic and the United States, so did music, hairstyles, and ideas of blackness and mixedness.[2] With local, regional, and international travel and migration, borders and nationness became more salient. We saw this with immigration to the Dominican Republic from Haiti and other Latin American and Caribbean countries as well as from the United States, Europe, and Asia. A nation once defined in one particular way can change over time as more people enter and leave its borders and as new ideas are introduced. I have focused here on the Dominican Republic as a case study to illustrate how such change takes place. In particular, I traced the importance of the idea of mixture (the *liga*) and used it as a point of entry to examine Dominicanness along the lines of mixture linking race, color, and nation in the articulation of Dominicanness. The socio-racial categories changed over time as Dominicans made new, and competing, claims about "who they were." All the while, color continued to be an important criterion in both the Dominican Republic and in the United States in the configuration of identities.

Dominicanness, Race, and Nation

This book examined the epistemological shift of blackness in the Dominican Republic (away from Haitians and toward African Americans). At the same time, this book explored the complexities surrounding the construction of racial identity and the ways in which Dominicanness, in both racial and national terms, was articulated over time in the Dominican Republic. I demonstrated how racial and national identities were reconfigured as people immigrated to and emigrated from the Dominican Republic. While categories have changed to some extent, the one constant current is the idea of mixture. Mixture was an important distinguishing feature as Haitians and Europeans immigrated to the Dominican Republic—as they were considered to represent "pure" racial groups (*negro* and *blanco*).

In the early twentieth century, as witnessed in Dominican newspapers, the idea of Dominican *gente de color* existed. During this time, there were three state-sanctioned racial groups (*blancos, mestizos,* and *negros*)—*mestizo* described the majority of the population in racial terms. Importantly, during this time, Dominicans were considered to be "of color." This changed with the promotion of *hispanidad* during the dictatorship of Rafael Trujillo as *hispanidad* moved away from the idea of being "of color" toward a more Spanish ideal. Race was conceptualized with a distance from blacks and Africans. *Hispanidad* embraced "all that was Spanish" and an appreciation of Spanish culture and society. Spain became the point of reference and a link to understanding Dominican life, people, and practices (for example, language and religion).

Mestizaje arose as a way to not only frame mixture in Dominican society but also as a way of describing a process of newness in a "biological" and cultural sense. *Hispanidad* cast an eye toward Spain while *mestizaje* explained encounters and resultant mixture. While there was an appreciation for Spanish influences and contributions to Dominican culture during the Trujillo regime, the Dominican Republic as homeland—the *patria*—emerged as one of Trujillo's legacies. The *patria* suggests that Dominicans are linked to a particular land or territory, a particular history, and *are* a particular "type" of people due to homogenization practices in imagining the nation. The claim "we are Dominican" emerges, linking people to a place at different points in time and linking race and nation in a way that *being Dominican* means having a generational presence, roots, and *liga* that is particular to the Dominican Republic.

Mulataje is one of the two emerging racial projects challenging *mestizaje*. It articulates a new racial view and reflects a *negro-blanco* (black-white) mixture with assertions of being *mulato*. The *mulato* category emerged in part due to the experiences of Dominicans in the United States with race and racial categorizations and the lack of an "in-between" category there. These experiences were combined with learning that *indio* has a different meaning in the United States and refers to different "types" of people such as Native Americans and people from India. Interactions with people and institutional structures that define Dominicans in new and different ways in the United States facilitate this process of *mulataje*.

The other racial project, *africanidad*, overlaps with *mulataje* in the sense that they both recognize African ancestry and emerged after Dominicans had experiences outside of the Dominican Republic that caused a "period of reflection." While *mulataje* is linked to the *mulato* socio-racial category, *africanidad* asserts a *negro* (black) and/or Afro-Dominican identity. The primary difference is that *mulataje* still captures a sense of racial "in-betweenness," while *africanidad* extends beyond mixture to address issues of ancestry and similarities throughout the African diaspora. These two related projects emerged during a time when Dominicans across borders were defined and defined themselves in different ways due to the contestation surrounding *indio* people who considered them to be black.

It has to be said that the Dominican Republic was not unique in its creation of mixed racial/color categories—they are evident throughout the Americas. What is especially interesting here, however, is that until 1998 the state created categories that were outside of the social history of the country in terms of insinuating Indian-Spanish mixture with the usage of *mestizo* and *indio*, for example. As discussed in the book, while members of the elite, at various points in time, were negrophobic, racialist thinking in the United States and elsewhere may have played a role in perpetuating racialist beliefs, especially during the early part of the twentieth when the U.S. Marines occupied both the Dominican Republic and Haiti. Strategically, the United States was in a position to make these distinctions between the Dominican Republic and Haiti.

Another point of interest in the Dominican racial system is the shift from race to color (demonstrated in the change in census categories) in that race mixture becomes a presumption—with resulting color variation. If race mixture is presumed, and if being mixed is a characteristic of Dominicanness, then historically and contemporaneously certain groups have been, and still are, excluded from this particular construction of nationness. Those groups defined as "pure" in the Dominican Republic, without much intermarriage and mixture, find themselves on the ends of a racial/color system that defines the majority of Dominicans as being distinct from these groups.

With the incorporation of different national groups over time, the Dominican national historical memory reflected competing views of history—with emphasis on the Spanish, the Taínos, or on the "encounters" between these and other groups. Because of the homogenizing efforts surrounding these histories, the African presence was, in effect, buried and erased from the historical record and memory—this is being unburied, however, at the present time. Several Dominican scholars and grass-roots organizations are working to unbury the African past and form alliances with Haiti and with other groups in the African diaspora.

Racial and National Identities in the Dominican Republic "on the Ground"

As discussed in the book, *mestizaje* has long been associated with nationness in Latin America and the Hispanic Caribbean. Defined as a process of race mixture, it suggests a starting point of newness. I illustrated how *mestizaje* became a foundational theme and a "given" in the Dominican Republic, where Dominicanness was defined in terms of newness and in terms of a long-standing history of mixture. The Dominican case illustrates a microlevel and place-specific process within a broader framework of *mestizaje*, which seeks to define certain mixtures that give rise to the processes of *mulataje* and *africanidad*. The issue then becomes one of interaction between local and global forces, the movement of people and ideas, and interactions between racial systems that have an impact on how people are making sense of *who they are* along the lines of race and nation with mixture as *a given*.

It can be said then that mixture is a distinguishing feature that links a sense of shared history and pastness, Dominican ancestry, with a sense of *being* and *feeling* Dominican. This has been translated into the construction of the terms *mestizo, indio,* and *mulato* and the subsequent configuration of "Dominican" national identity along the lines of color and mixedness. *Mestizaje* espoused a non-white, non-black, "in-between" identity; thus, while most Dominicans would not say they are black, they also would not say they are white. This is the point of the *liga*—it represents a combination or mixture and the sense of a "new" people. However, the *liga* and articulations of Dominicanness will continue to change as long as people and ideas continue to cross borders and interact with other people and different racial systems, thus redefining the system and its categories while being defined by the system and other actors, and as Domican scholars and activists critically engage representations of the past.

Racial and national identities are often connected in the expressed consensus that *indio* was "invented" in the Dominican Republic and is tied to *being Dominican* in a national sense. In this way, the configuration of Dominicans as a "mixed" people is then characterized by the in-between category of *indio*. As I have presented here, *indio* as a concept and category has been contested by people who have reflected on their own identities as a result of experiences abroad or through rethinking the course of history in the Dominican Republic.

The more historically "accurate" category, *mulato*, officially entered the Dominican racial discourse with its inclusion on the *cédula* in 1998 and due to individual claims of being *mulato*. Despite this, however, there is still resistance to it because it connotes African ancestry and blackness. There is also resistance because *indio* has a long history in the Dominican Republic and social and cultural significance. I think, however, that *mulato* will gain more widespread acceptance in the Dominican Republic within the next few years simply because of the consensus that "*indio* does not exist" and because of the need to replace it with something that captures a racial in-between status. In addition to *mulato*, others may continue to advance the idea of *mestizo* instead of *indio*, and Identidad and other groups may work to advance "Afro-Dominican." Without doubt, there are a number of agentive forces in place that are challenging existent categories and how they articulate the sense of being Dominican.

Some Dominican scholars are examining issues surrounding identity by reviewing historical claims and making new assertions about the need to revise history and develop a more accurate presentation of the past and its relationship to the present with respect to Haiti as well as the identities and the socio-racial categories that are used.[3] In March 2004, UNESCO sponsored an international interdisciplinary seminar called La Ruta del Esclavo on the Atlantic African slave trade and its consequences in Santo Domingo. I had the opportunity to meet other researchers and scholars from the Dominican Republic, other areas of the Caribbean, and the United States to discuss issues surrounding the slave trade as well as its impact. This is but one example of how issues of *africanidad* (Africanity) are being positioned and discussed in the Dominican Republic (see fig. 4.6).

In addition to the scholarship on this topic, Dominican organizations have formed in an effort to organize around the issues of identity and coalition building with Haitians and other people of African descent. Identidad is one of the primary organizations involved in this consciousness-raising effort, along with Women of the Altagracia Church in Santiago, the Coordinadora de Mujeres de Cibao (Women's Coordinating Effort of Cibao), Nucleo de Apoyo a la Mujer (Center for the Support of Women) in Santiago, and the organization Onè Respe. They all work to combat racism and some create a coalition with Haitians. Together, all of the organizations working in tandem are helping to situate the Dominican Republic in the Caribbean and in the African Diaspora as they unbury the African past.

Appendixes

Appendix A. Santiago Population Census by Gender, 1903

National Groups by Gender	Population
Dominican Men	4,775
Dominican Women	5,624
Spanish Men	60
Spanish Women	31
French Men	4
French Women	7
English Men	3
English Women	0
German Men	1
German Women	0
Belgian Men	1
Belgian Women	0
Danish Men	2
Danish Women	1
Dutch Men	2
Dutch Women	1
Italian Men	33
Italian Women	0
Arab Men	113
Arab Women	80
Chinese Men	2
Chinese Women	0
American Men	64
American Women	28
Cuban Men	23
Cuban Women	13
Haitian Men	31
Haitian Women	20
Venezuelan Men	1
Venezuelan Women	1
Mexican Men	1
Mexican Women	1

Source: 1903 Census of Santiago. Archivo Histórico de Santiago. Translated as presented by Kimberly Eison Simmons.

Note: Appendix A clearly shows the diversity that existed in Santiago during the early 1900s, with attention to nationality and gender.

Appendix B. 1916 Santiago Census

Santiago de los Caballeros
Total Population in Santiago 14,774

Gender		Nationality		Religion	
Women	Men	Dominican	Foreign	Catholic	Other
8,077	6,697	13,167	1,607	14,303	471

Note: Appendix B represents the gender, nationality, and religious background of the population in Santiago in 1916, thirteen years after the first Santiago census.

Appendix C. Nationality of Resident Foreigners in the City of Santiago de los Caballeros in 1916

Nationality	Population
North American	692
Haitian	388
Arab	184
Puerto Rican	104
Spanish	60
Italian	49
English	37
Chinese	21
French	18
Cuban	16
Belgian	13
German	10
Venezuelan	5
Danish	4
Dutch	3
Colombian	2
Mexican	1
TOTAL	1,607

Source: Archivo Histórico de Santiago. Compiled and translated by Kimberly Eison Simmons.

Appendix D. Race in the First National Census, 1920

Total Population 894,665

Racial Category	Number	Percentage
Blancos/White (Dominicans and Foreigners)	223,144	24.9
Mestizos/Mixed (Including *Amarillos*/Asians)	444,587	49.7
Negros/Black (Including 28,258 Haitians)	226,934	25.4

Note: Generally in the provinces, the number of whites in the cities is higher than in the *campo* (rural area). Haitians account for 3.2 percent of the population. Compiled and translated by Kimberly Eison Simmons.

Appendix E. "We Need Immigrants"

The following commentary was published in 1930 with the heading "We Need Immigrants" and articulates the "need" for a certain "type" of immigrants.

. . . Como no podemos traer todos esos inmigrantes, de un sólo golpe, podríamos, en cambio, seleccionar un grupo de ellos y dar principio en seguida, sin fabulosos gastos, a la obra de poblar nuestro suelo de gente sana, honrada y trabajadora, tan necesaria para aumentar la riqueza el poder y el bienestar de nuestra Patria.

Y de ninguna parte podríamos traer mejor gente que de España. El inmigrante español, por afinidad de raza, religión e idioma, es el que mejor liga hace con nuestro pueblo, y es, por lo tanto, el que más nos conviene.

No hablaremos más del importante problema de que nos libraría automáticamente el fomento de esta inmigración. No hablaremos de que ella evitaría la lamentable despoblación de nuestra tierra, para pasar a hacer una consideración de otro importante mal de que nos libraría también la llegada al país del elemento sano y tabajador [*sic*] de que venimos hablando.

Este mal, es la lamentable "haitianización" de que estamos siendo víctimas. Todos saben que la inmigración haitiana ha llegado a tomar tal incremento, que constituye un peligro cierto para nuestra personalidad latina, para la fisonomía de nuestro pueblo, para la Patria, en fin, dejando a un lado las insinuaciones Pues bien [*sic*]; sabido esto, sale al paso en seguida una de las más apreciables ventajas de la inmigración a que primero nos referimos. Poniendo a estos inmigrantes como barrera en los campos cercanos a nuestro límite occidental, queda suprimida la invasión.

Source: El Diario, January 15, 1930, from the Lineas Editoriales section entitled "Necesitamos Inmigrantes," front page. Archivo Histórico de Santiago.

(. . . Since we cannot bring all those immigrants, at one time, we could, however, select a group of them quickly, without much expense, working to populate our land of healthy, honest, and hard-working people, as it is necessary to increase the wealth, the power, and the well-being of our Homeland.

And there is no other place we could bring a better people than from Spain. The Spanish immigrant, for likeness of race, religion, and language, is the best combination with our people, and, therefore, is the one that we need.

We won't speak anymore of the important problem this would automatically liberate us from [as] a result of this immigration. We won't mention that it would prevent the unfortunate depopulation of our land, to continue to make a consideration of the importance that we would be liberated by the arrival in our country of the healthy element and work ethic that we are talking about.

This bad [situation] is the unfortunate "haitianizacion" that we are falling victim to. Everyone knows that the Haitian immigration, over time, has created certain danger for our Latin personality, for the physical features of our community, for the Homeland, in short, now then leaving aside the insinuations; knowing this, let's move quickly toward the advantages of the immigration to which we first referred. By placing these immigrants as barriers in the rural areas near our western border, the invasion is suppressed.

Appendix F. Desired Immigration

Below is my translation of a memo written by Trujillo in 1939 discussing "desired" immigration and the "need" to "whiten" certain areas that are "too dark":

The Supreme Boss and Director
of the Dominican Party
Memo
The Honorable Mr. President of
the Republic

It is evident that the populations located in or close to the border need injection of new blood, especially of the white race.

I recommend that the Secretaries of State of the Interior and of Agriculture, Industry and Work make an agreement to send to those populations those people of Jewish race or foreigners of other races that want to leave to work in agriculture as branches of trade. They could also send professionals, doctors, etc. who could cooperate in the rising of the level of those populations in that to patriotism and development of their natural wealth it is necessary.

I believe that this can be very beneficial to the Dominican Republic, and I also believe that the Government should lend every type of help in the gradual development of this plan, the one which [I] allow myself to recommend to the consideration and comprehension of the gentleman President of the Republic.

Rafael L. Trujillo
Ciudad Trujillo,
April 3, 1939

Rafael Trujillo Memo. Published in Vega 1986, 145.

Appendix G. National Population Census, May 13, 1935

Total Inhabitants		1,479,417
Dominicans		1,406,347
Foreigners: All Races		73,070
Haitians:		
Urban Zones	Men:	1,571
	Women:	1,436 (3,007 total in Urban Zones)
Rural Zones	Men:	30,748
	Women:	18,902 (49,650 total in Rural Zones)
		Total: 52,657

Source: 1935 Census. Archivo Histórico de Santiago. Translated by Kimberly Eison Simmons.

Appendix H. Jewish Immigration to the Dominican Republic

The sad destiny of thousands and thousands of human beings, stripped of their properties, harassed from their homes, mistreated, tortured, and sent to extermination camps, prompted the President of the United States of America, Franklin D. Roosevelt, to convoke in the year 1938 an International Conference to discuss the immigrant Jews, in the city of Evian, France.

Thirty-two countries sent delegations. The result was depressing; none showed willingness to admit the Jews that were left without a country.

Only the delegation from the Dominican Republic declared that their country was willing to give protection to One Hundred Thousand refugees, victims of the Nazi persecution.

The Dominican Republic let the doors open to save thousands of innocent lives from the holocaust in Europe.

The noble gesture of its government and people constitutes a historic event of the XXth Century.

Meanwhile, at the other side of the Atlantic Ocean efforts were being made to make the promise a significant event, a reality.

After many meetings held in 1939, the American Jewish Joint Agricultural Corporation (AGRO-Joint) takes charge and supplies the initial capital to start the project and so the base for the foundation of the Dominican Republic Settlement Association, Inc. (called *La Dorsa*) has been formed.

On January of the year 1940 Dr. James N. Rosenberg, President of La DORSA, moves to the Dominican Republic and on January 30,

1940 the Dominican Government signs an Agreement, ratified immediately by the National Congress.

The Generalísimo Dr. Rafael Leonidas Trujillo Molina donated 26,000 acres of his property in Sosúa, in the Northern coast of the country, in the name of the Dominican Republic and as a personal contribution for a humanitarian project.

Source: Sosúa: From Refuge to Paradise (Eichen 1995, 7–8).

Appendix I. Race and Color in Comparison, 1935 and 1950 Census, Combined Dominicans and Foreigners

Color	1935	1950
Blanco (White)	192,733	600,994
Negro (Black)	287,677	245,032
Mestizo (Mixed)	998,668	1,289,285
Amarillo (Asian)	339	561

Source: Archivo Histórico de Santiago. Compiled and translated by Kimberly Eison Simmons.

Appendix J. First Language, 1950 Census

First Language	Total	Men	Women
La República/The Dominican Republic (Total)	2,135,872	1,070,742	1,065,130
Spanish	2,093,195	1,043,760	1,049,525
Arabic	1,978	1,100	878
French	25,405	16,747	8,658
English	12,140	7,288	4,852
Italian	562	372	190
Other	2,578	1,554	1,024
Unknown	14	11	3

Source: Archivo Histórico de Santiago. Compiled and translated by Kimberly Eison Simmons.

Appendix K. Religion, 1935 and 1950 National Censuses

Religion	1935	1950
La República/The Dominican Republic (Total)	1,479,417	2,135,872
Catholic	1,458,790	2,098,474
Protestant	15,384	30,538
Buddhist	0	56
Jewish	0	463
Adventist	0	2,902
Other	5,243	1,356
None	0	1,845
None Declared	0	238

Source: Archivo Histórico de Santiago. Compiled and translated by Kimberly Eison Simmons.

Appendix L. Trujillo Memos

Below is a memo from a collection published by Bernardo Vega, a Dominican scholar and former ambassador to the United States. It articulates Dominicanization along the lines of race, nationality, and language.

Dominican Republic
Secretary of State of the Interior and Police
Cuidad Trujillo, D.S.D.
July 9, 1943
To: Mr. Secretary of State of the Presidency,
Your Office.
Matter: Measures to prevent Kreyol from being spoken in the border region of the Dominican Republic.
Ref.: Number 10304, dated May 7

1.—In relation to your attentive engagement to this matter, I would like to inform you that, in spite of the fact that the Secretary of State has carried out a careful and detailed study about the possibility of preventing the spread of and avoiding the usage of Kreyol in the border region of the Dominican Republic, he found that neither legal nor administrative means is possible at the present time to prevent the use of this dialect.

2.—The desire expressed by his Excellency Mr. President of the Republic to banish the use of a strange language in the border region in absolute to our language, that is recommended for its high patriotic sense. We understand, however, that it could be obtained as a result of a didactic and educational effort.

Very sincerely,

M. A. Pena Batille,

Secretary of State of the Interior and Police

M. A. Peña Batille Memo. Published in Vega 1986, 140. Translated by Kimberly Eison Simmons.

Notes

Introduction: Burying the African Past

1. See http://www.miamiherald.com/multimedia/news/afrolatin/part2/index. html.

2. I use light- and dark-skinned as well as light- and dark-complexioned to talk about skin color diversity in the African American community.

Chapter 1. Stirring the *Sancocho*: Dominicanness, Race, and Mixture in Historical Context

1. Marrying up refers to the practice of choosing a mate or partner who has a lighter skin tone with the idea of "lightening" the next generation.

2. *Mestizo* was first used as a racial category but later referred to color on the Dominican national census. I suspect that this shift was in concert with claims of racial democracy throughout the region (for example, in Brazil and Venezuela). Even with the shift, *mestizo* still functioned as a racial category because it represented "mixed race" people. Contemporaneously, *indio* refers to skin color but also functions as a racial category.

3. When *indio* is not used to describe color, terms such as *trigueño* (wheat colored) and *moreno* (brown) are used.

4. This section is based on a paper I gave in 1996 at the 95th Annual AAA meetings in San Francisco, entitled "There Is No Racial Democracy Here: Exploring Afro-Venezuelan (Re)Emerging 'Community of Consciousness' and Action" (with Dr. Ruth Simms Hamilton as co-author).

5. During this time, President Jean Pierre Boyer of Haiti wrote a message to José Núñez de Cáceres, then the leader of the Dominican Republic, indicating that he had made the necessary preparations to unite the island; this was against the backdrop of the imminent French invasion entering from the Dominican Republic side (Moya Pons 1995, 122). Cáceres did not want unification but felt he couldn't win; despite resistance, Boyer soon became the leader of the entire island but resigned in 1843 because of growing tension and revolts, seeking exile in Jamaica (139).

6. While the majority of Dominicans were defined as *mestizo*, I choose to describe them as *mulato* within the context of this historical period. The combination *mestizo/mulato* here represents their category along with my own.

7. See Nelson 1988, Hoetink 1982, and Moya Pons 1995 for an in-depth account and analysis of the Spanish-descended Creole emigration from the Dominican Republic.

8. This is based on a review of the literature giving historical accounts or demographic information about the population.

9. This particular advertisement was for a hair product on May 20, 1918 (running on numerous days) in *El Diario* (The Daily) in Santiago. The newspaper is no longer in circulation.

10. "El Diario" is followed by "Santiago de los Caballeros, República Dominicana, W.I." (taken from the masthead in 1918).

11. This census predates the first national census in 1920. See Hoetink 1982 for more of a historical description of transnational migration during this time period.

12. See Moya Pons 1995 for an in-depth account of the occupation.

13. See Hoetink 1982, Knight 1978, Rout 1976, and E. Williams 1970 for a more thorough discussion of migration throughout the Caribbean.

14. This is my new area of research, focusing on the founding of the Brown Fellowship Society, its legacy in the southern United States, and politics of color in the African American community today.

15. I have chosen to keep *indio* in Spanish and not translate it into "Indian" (direct English translation) since that is not the connotative meaning of *indio* among Dominicans.

16. From reading declassified documents (from the U.S. Department of State), it is evident that the United States maintained a relationship with Trujillo (after the U.S. military occupation ended and into Trujillo's presidency).

17. At this time the importance of quantifying Haitians along the lines of gender and in both rural and urban areas grew. For the first time, in the 1935 census summary, the Haitian population data is prominently placed after Dominicans and foreigners, drawing attention to the numbers and the overall presence of Haitians in the Dominican Republic (see appendix G).

18. Many participants in my study expressed these views of Haitians and the "racist" treatment that Haitians received in Santiago.

19. Dominican and Dominico-Haitian organizations are working to help improve the social and economic condition of Haitians in the Dominican Republic.

20. The idea that Haitians were, and are, closely associated with Africa, African practices, and blackness was prevalent throughout my interviews with the participants in my study.

21. The tensions between the Dominican Republic and Haiti were difficult to ignore. The United States and neighboring countries (for example, Mexico and Cuba) were aware of these tensions. In a letter to President Franklin D. Roosevelt, Rafael Trujillo wrote, "My Government will concur in the conciliation procedure initiated by Haiti with the same desire it has always cherished of giving the Government and people of Haiti the most complete satisfaction with regard to any legitimate claim that they may present on the ground of the regrettable and regretted incidents that occurred in the Dominican territory early in October." In his response to Trujillo, President Roosevelt wrote, "Permit me further to express my gratification by reason of Your Excellency's statement that the Government of the Dominican Republic will

not give the slightest ground for a disturbance of the peace of America, in the preservation of which all the peoples of the New World have so great and legitimate an interest. I extend to Your Excellency my most sincere wishes that the controversy which regrettably exists between two sister republics may obtain a rapid, just, and pacific solution through the utilization of the inter-American peace instruments to which they have now announced their determination to have recourse." It was clear from the declassified State Department documents that President Roosevelt maintained communication with the president of Haiti and other heads of state in the region about the "controversy" and possible "disturbance" in the region.

22. The following definitions are from the 1950 national census regarding color and nationality. At a glance, the enumerator recorded the color of the person being interviewed, but in situations where color was not "obvious," the person was asked about his or her color. This is the first time that a definition appeared on the census defining color in this way.

Chapter 2. *Indio*: A Question of Color

1. The *cédula* can be issued to sixteen year olds (with no voting rights until they reach eighteen). This particular *cédula* was valid until 2004.

2. This is from an interview with Celia on August 4, 1998.

3. I have chosen to leave *indio* in Spanish because of its connotative meaning.

4. The afternoon lunch and siesta follow a Spanish tradition, although this is changing slightly since more people have to work (as more grocery and specialty shops stay open during the lunch period).

5. Nelsa helped us around the house on occasion for about five months in 1998.

Chapter 3. The Dominican Diaspora: Blackening and Whitening and Mixture across Borders

1. When I was in the Dominican Republic in the summer of 2008, I was told that *El Siglo* was no longer in circulation.

2. Maria Filomena Gonzalez, a friend and colleague in Santo Domingo, has been working with a team appointed by the Department of Education to revise school textbooks.

3. Crossing the border is more difficult now; the process has become more systematized and Dominicans should carry a passport to cross the border in Dajabón. A passport was necessary to spend time in Haiti. For years, a passport has been required to cross the border in the South (going to Port-au-Prince and other locations in the South).

4. Dominican–African American social interaction and racialized experiences in the United States demonstrate one way in which Dominican racialization is challenged. In addition, some Dominican scholars challenge long-held ideas about Dominicanness based on their own research and reflection on history.

Chapter 4. *Africanidad* and Afro-Dominican: Alliances, Organizations, and Networks in the African Diaspora

1. Chiqui made this comment during her presentation at the poetry reading.

2. I offered to be an ally and to help the group tell its story, to facilitate the visibility of Identidad in the Dominican Republic and in the United States, and to assist it in ways that would contribute to its growth and sustainability as an organization (for example, identifying funding sources, participating in workshops, donating magazines that deal with African American women's issues, and so forth).

3. I translated these objectives from some of Identidad's earlier publications for the AAA and AES paper presentations.

4. This is my translation from an interview with Ochy.

5. In Casa por la Identidad de las Mujeres Afro, "Memorias del Taller Sobre Estrategias y Metodologias para Combatir el Racismo" (Memories of a Presentation about Strategies and Methodologies to Combat Racism), Santo Domingo, 1998.

6. This quote by Galvan is from the paper she presented at the meeting in Costa Rica.

7. The excerpt is taken from *Cimarrona* 2(7) (October 1998): 1.

Conclusion. Unburying the African Past

1. On a personal note, I have experienced much of what I explore here in this book—shifts in personal and group identity categories, migration and living abroad, reconstructing racial and color identities, having one foot "here" and the other "there" because of research, family, and a connection to place, and working with scholars and activists to build alliances in the African Diaspora. When I left the Dominican Republic in 2004, it was to be closer to family in the United States and to work at the University of South Carolina in anthropology and African American studies. My oldest daughter went through first grade in the Dominican Republic, and my two other children were born there, and they all claim "Dominican" as *part* of their heritage because of their time and experience there. From 1993 to the present, I have experienced life in the Dominican Republic as a student, professor, researcher, mother, wife, colleague, neighbor, friend, godmother, and *co-madre*. We were—and continue to be—part of a wonderful community.

2. As I completed the book project, I returned to the Dominican Republic in the summers of 2007 and 2008. Both times, I noticed more representations of Afro-Dominicanness—of being Afro-Dominican, *mulato/a*, and/or black—as expressed not only in terms of personal identity, but also in dress and hairstyles and in popular music. In 2007, as I sat in the airport in Miami waiting to board the plane to Santiago, I noticed several young and teenage boys dressed in baggy pants and large shirts with short faded haircuts (also a popular haircut for African American boys). As I looked around the area, I noticed an older teenage boy with corn-rolled (braided) hair and many people who *appeared* to be African American (because of hair and clothing

styles typically associated with African Americans). Some were speaking Spanish and others were speaking English and talking about going to Dominican Republic on summer vacation to visit friends and family. Others were returning home. In some cases, it was hard to know *who* was Dominican and *who* was African American. Mutual influencing of Dominicans and African Americans was apparent in fashion and hairstyle (curly or straight style). Some of this shared sense of style—especially among the younger generation—is a reflection of hip-hop culture, music, and fashion. Also, during these two summers, I noticed more women with curly, braided, and short natural hairstyles and teenage boys with corn-rolled hair in both Santiago and Santo Domingo. In a park in Santo Domingo one afternoon, I saw a group of teenage boys with long dreadlocks wearing Bob Marley t-shirts. As we rode around Santo Domingo, I noticed a sign for a beauty salon with a photo of Beyoncé (with straight hair with big curls). On a trip to the North Coast I was struck by all of the new development projects targeting Europeans and Americans. West Indies Real Estate specializes in real estate properties on the North Coast and had large signs advertising apartment buildings and condominiums for sale.

    3. Such works include Záiter Mejía 1996; Mateo 1996; Andújar Persinal 2004, 1997; Franco Pichardo 1997, 1989; Vega et al. 1997; Tejeda Ortiz 1998; Albert Batista 1993; Identidad 1997; Onè Respe 1995; Manuel Madruga 1986; Silié 1976; and Jiménez 1996.

References

Books and Journals

Adams, Robert. 2006. "History at the Crossroads: Vodú and the Modernization of the Dominican Borderlands." In *Globalization and Race: Transformations in the Cultural Production of Blackness*, ed. Kamari Maxine Clarke and Deborah A. Thomas, 55–72. Durham, N.C.: Duke University Press.

Albert Batista, Celsa. 1993. *Mujer y Esclavitud en Santo Domingo*. Santo Domingo: Editora Búho.

Alvarez, Julia. 1993. "Black Behind the Ears." *Essence* (February): 42, 129.

Anderson, Benedict. 1983. *Imagined Communities: Reflections on the Origin and Spread of Nationalism*. London: Verso.

Andújar Persinal, Carlos. 2004. *Identidad Cultural y Religiosidad Popular*. Santo Domingo: Editorial Letra Gráfica.

———. 1997. *La Presencia Negra en Santo Domingo*. Santo Domingo: Impresora Búho.

Aparicio, Ana. 2006. *Dominican-Americans and the Politics of Empowerment*. Gainesville: University Press of Florida.

Austerlitz, Paul. 1997. *Merengue: Dominican Music and Dominican Identity*. Philadelphia: Temple University Press.

Baker, Lee. 1998. *From Savage to Negro: Anthropology and the Construction of Race 1896–1954*. Berkeley: University of California Press.

Basch, Linda, Nina Glick Schiller, and Christina Szanton Blanc. 1994. *Nations Unbound: Transnational Projects, Postcolonial Predicaments, and Deterritorialized Nation-States*. Amsterdam: Gordon and Breach Publishers.

Blakey, Michael L. 1994. "Passing the Buck: Naturalism and Individualism as Anthropological Expressions of Euro-American Denial." In *Race*, ed. Steven Gregory and Roger Sanjek, 270–84. New Brunswick, N.J.: Rutgers University Press.

Betances, Emelio. 1995. *State and Society in the Dominican Republic*. Boulder, Colo.: Westview Press.

Brennan, Denise. 2004. *What's Love Got to Do with It?: Transnational Desires and Sex Tourism in the Dominican Republic*. Durham, N.C.: Duke University Press.

Caldwell, Kia Lilly. 2007. *Negras in Brazil: Re-envisioning Black Women, Citizenship, and the Politics of Identity*. New Brunswick, N.J.: Rutgers University Press.

Candelario, Ginetta E. B. 2007. *Black Behind the Ears: Dominican Racial Identity from Museums to Beauty Shops*. Durham, N.C.: Duke University Press.

———. 2004. "Voices from Hispaniola: A Meridians Roundtable with Edwidge Danticat, Loida Maritza Pérez, Myriam J. A. Chancy, and Nelly Rosario." *Meridians: Feminism, Race, Transnationalism* 5(1): 69–91.

———. 2001. "'Black Behind the Ears'—and Up Front Too? Dominicans in the Black Mosaic." *Public Historian* (Fall) 23(4): 55–73.

Cassá, Roberto. 1975. "El Racismo en la Ideología de la Clase Dominante Dominicana." *Ciencia* 3(1): 59–85.

Craig, Maxine Leeds. 2002. *Ain't I a Beauty Queen?: Black Women, Beauty, and the Politics of Race.* New York: Oxford University Press.

Davis, F. James. 1991. *Who Is Black? One Nation's Definition.* University Park: Pennsylvania State University Press.

Davis, Martha Ellen. 1994. "'Bi-Musicality' in the Cultural Configurations of the Caribbean." *Black Music Research Journal* (14)2: 145–60.

———. 1983. "Cantos de Esclavos y Libertos: Cancionero de Anthems (Coros) de Samana." *Boletín del Museo del Hombre Dominicano* 18: 197–236.

———. 1981. "La Cultura Musical Religiosa de los 'Americanos' de Samana." *Boletín del Museo del Hombre Dominicano* 15: 127–69.

Derby, Lauren. 2000. "The Dictator's Seduction: Gender and State Spectacle during the Trujillo Regime." *Callaloo* 23(3): 1112–46.

———. 1994. "Haitians, Magic, and Money: Raza and Society in the Haitian-Dominican Borderlands, 1900 to 1937." *Comparative Studies in Society and History* (36)3: 488–526.

Derby, Robin L. H., and Richard Turits. 1993. "Historias de Terror y los Terrors de la Historia: La Masacre Haitiana de 1937 en la República Dominicana." *Estudios Sociales* 26(92): 65–76.

Domínguez, Virginia. 1994. *White by Definition: Social Classification in Creole Louisiana.* New Brunswick, N.J.: Rutgers University Press.

Dore Cabral, Carlos. 1987. "Los Dominicanos de Origen Haitiano y la Segregación Social en la República Dominicana." *Estudios Sociales* 20(68): 57–80.

Duany, Jorge. 2002. *The Puerto Rican Nation on the Move: Identities on the Island and in the United States.* Chapel Hill: University of North Carolina Press.

———. 1998. "Reconstructing Racial Identity: Ethnicity, Color, and Class among Dominicans in the United States and Puerto Rico." *Latin American Perspectives* 25(3): 147–72.

———. 1994. *Quisqueya on the Hudson: The Transnational Identity of Dominicans in Washington Heights.* Dominican Research Monographs. New York: CUNY Dominican Studies Institute.

———. 1985. "Ethnicity in the Spanish Caribbean: Notes on the Consolidation of Creole Identity in Cuba and Puerto Rico, 1762–1868." *Ethnic Groups* 6: 99–123.

Eichen, Josef David. 1995. *Sosúa: From Refuge to Paradise.* Trans. J. Armando Bermúdez. Santo Domingo: Amigo del Hogar.

Featherstone, Mike. 1995. *Undoing Culture: Globalization, Postmodernism, and Identity.* London: Sage Publications.

Foner, Nancy. 2002. *From Ellis Island to JFK: New York's Two Great Waves of Immigration.* New Haven, Conn.: Yale University Press.

Foster, Robert J. 1991. "Making National Cultures in the Global Ecumene." *Annual Review of Anthropology* 20: 235–60.

Franco Pichardo, Franklin J. 1997. *Sobre Racismo y Antihaitianismo (y Otros Ensayos).* Santo Domingo: Impresora Vidal.

———. 1989. *Los Negros, Los Mulatos y la Nación Dominicana.* Santo Domingo: Editora Nacional.

Friedman, Jonathan. 1994. *Cultural Identity and Global Process.* London: Sage Publications.

Galvan, Sergia. 1995. "Power, Racism, and Identity." In *Connecting Across Cultures and Continents: Black Women Speak Out on Identity, Race, and Development,* ed. Achola O. Pala, 47–52. New York: UNIFEM.

Georges, Eugenia. 1990. *The Making of a Transnational Community: Migration, Development, and Cultural Change in the Dominican Republic.* New York: Columbia University Press.

Godreau, Isar P. 2002. "Changing Space, Making Race: Distance, Nostalgia, and the Folklorization of Blackness in Puerto Rico." *Identities* 3 (July-September): 281–304.

Grasmuck, Sherri, and Patricia R. Pessar. 1991. *Between Two Islands: Dominican International Migration.* Berkeley: University of California Press.

Gregory, Steven. 2006. *The Devil behind the Mirror: Globalization and Politics in the Dominican Republic.* Berkeley: University of California Press.

Guarnizo, Luis E. 1994. "Los Dominicanyorks: The Making of a Binational Society." *Annals of the American Academy of Political and Social Science* 533: 77–78.

Hamilton, Ruth Simms. 2007. *Routes of Passage: Rethinking the African Diaspora.* East Lansing: Michigan State University Press.

———. 1990. *Creating a Paradigm and Research Agenda for Comparative Studies of the Worldwide Dispersion of African Peoples.* East Lansing: Michigan State Press.

Harrison, Faye. 1995. "The Persistent Power of 'Race' in the Cultural and Political Economy of Racism." *Annual Review of Anthropology* 24: 47–74.

Hendricks, Glenn. 1974. *The Dominican Diaspora: From the Dominican Republic to New York City—Villagers in Transition.* New York: Teachers College Press, Columbia University.

Hoetink, Harry. 1982. *The Dominican People, 1850–1900: Notes for a Historical Sociology.* Baltimore: Johns Hopkins University Press.

———. 1967. *Caribbean Race Relations: A Study of Two Variants.* New York: Walker.

Hoffnung-Garskof, Jesse. 2007. *A Tale of Two Cities: Santo Domingo and New York after 1950.* Princeton, N.J.: Princeton University Press.

Howard, David. 2001. *Coloring the Nation: Race and Ethnicity in the Dominican Republic.* Boulder, Colo.: L. Rienner Publishers.

Hunter, Margaret L. 2005. *Race, Gender, and the Politics of Skin Tone*. New York: Routledge.

Identidad (Casa por la Identidad de las Mujeres Afro). 1997. *Memoria del Foro: Por una Sociedad Libre de Prejuicio Racial*. Santo Domingo: Editora Búho.

Itzigsohn, José, and Carlos Dore-Cabral. 2000. "Competing Identities? Race, Ethnicity, and Panethnicity among Dominicans in the United States." *Sociological Forum* 15(2): 225–47.

Jiménez, Blas. 1996. *El Nativo (Versos en Cuentos para Espantar Zombies)*. Santo Domingo: Editora Búho.

Kearney, Michael. 1995. "The Local and the Global: The Anthropology of Globalization and Transnationalism." *Annual Review of Anthropology* 24: 547–65.

Knight, Franklin W. 1978. *The Caribbean: The Genesis of a Fragmented Nationalism*. New York: Oxford University Press.

Kondo, Dorinne. 1990. *Crafting Selves: Power, Gender, and Discourses of Identity in a Japanese Workplace*. Chicago: University of Chicago Press.

Lamb, David. 1994. *Do Platanos Go Wit' Collard Greens?* New York: I Write What I Like Inc.

Levitt, Peggy. 2001. *The Transnational Villagers*. Berkeley: University of California Press.

Long, Norman. 1996. "Globalization and Localization: New Challenges to Rural Research." In *The Future of Anthropological Knowledge*, ed. Henrietta L. Moore, 37–59. New York: Routledge.

Manuel Madruga, José. 1986. *Azucar y Haitianos en la República Dominicana*. Santo Domingo: Editora Amigo del Hogar.

Martínez, Samuel. 1999. "From Hidden Hand to Heavy Hand: Sugar, the State, and Migrant Labor in Haiti and the Dominican Republic." *Latin American Research Review* 34(1): 57–84.

Martínez-Alier, Verena. 1989. *Marriage, Class, and Colour in Nineteenth-Century Cuba: A Study of Racial Attitudes and Sexual Values in a Slave Society*. Ann Arbor: University of Michigan Press.

Martínez-Echazábal, Lourdes. 1998. "Mestizaje and the Discourse of National/Cultural Identity in Latin America, 1845–1959." *Latin American Perspectives: Race and National Identity in the Americas* 25(3): 21–42.

Martínez-Vergne, Teresita. 2005. *Nation and Citizen in the Dominican Republic, 1880–1916*. Chapel Hill: University of North Carolina Press.

Mateo, Andrés L. 1996. *Al Filo de la Dominicanidad*. Santo Domingo: Librería la Trinitaria.

Mayes, April J. Forthcoming 2009. "Tolerating Sex: Prostitution, Gender, and Governance in the Dominican Republic, 1880s–1924." In *Health and Medicine in the Caribbean: Historical Perspectives*, ed. Juanita De Barros, Steven Palmer, and David Wright, chapter 6. New York and London: Routledge Press.

———. 2008. "Why Dominican Feminism Moved to the Right: Class, Colour, and

Women's Activism in the Dominican Republic, 1880s–1940s." *Gender and History* 20(2): 349–71.

Medina, Laurie Kroshus. 1997. "Defining Difference, Forging Unity: The Co-Construction of Race, Ethnicity, and Nation in Belize." *Ethnic and Racial Studies* 20(4): 757–80.

Minority Rights Group, eds. 1995. *No Longer Invisible: Afro-Latin Americans Today*. Co-edited by Pedro Pérez-Sarduy and Jean Stubbs. London: Minority Rights Group Publications.

Mintz, Sidney W. 1971. "Groups, Group Boundaries, and the Perception of Race." *Comparative Studies in Society and History* 13: 437–43.

Moya Pons, Frank. 1998. *The Dominican Republic: A National History*. Princeton, N.J.: Markus Wiener Publishers.

———. 1995. *The Dominican Republic: A National History*. New Rochelle, N.Y.: Hispaniola

Nelson, William Javier. 1988. "Dominican Creole Emigration: 1791–1861." Centro de Investigaciones del Caribe y América Latina (Caribbean Institute and Study Center for Latin America—CISCLA). Working Paper Series 32. San Germán: Inter-American University of Puerto Rico.

Oboler, Suzanne. 1995. *Ethnic Labels, Latino Lives: Identity and the Politics of (Re) Presentation in the United States*. Minneapolis: University of Minnesota Press.

Omi, Michael, and Howard Winant. 1994. *Racial Formation in the United States from the 1960s to the 1990s*. 2nd ed. New York: Routledge.

Onè Respe. 1995. *El Otro del Nosotros*. Santo Domingo: Editora Búho.

Ong, Aihwa. 1996. "Cultural Citizenship as Subject-Making: Immigrants Negotiate Racial and Cultural Boundaries in the United States." *Current Anthropology* 37(5): 737–62.

Pala, Achola A. 1995. *Connecting Across Cultures and Continents: Black Women Speak Out on Identity, Race, and Development*. New York: UNIFEM.

Paulino, Edward. 2005. "Erasing the Kreyol from the Margins of the Dominican Republic: The Pre- and Post-Nationalist Project of the Border, 1930–1945." *Wadabagei* 8(2): 35–71.

Pessar, Patricia R. 1996. *A Visa for a Dream: Dominicans in the United States*. Boston: Allyn and Bacon.

Rahier, Jean Muteba. 2003. "Introduction: Mestizaje, Mulataje, Mestiçagem in Latin American Ideologies of National Identities." *Journal of Latin American Anthropology* 8(1): 40–50.

Rodriguez, Clara E. 2000. *Changing Race: Latinos, the Census, and the History of Ethnicity*. New York: New York University Press.

Roediger, David. 2006. *Working Toward Whiteness: How America's Immigrants Became White; The Strange Journey from Ellis Island to the Suburbs*. New York: Basic Books.

Rooks, Noliwe M. 1996. *Hair Raising: Beauty, Culture, and African American Women*. New Brunswick, N.J.: Rutgers University Press.

Rosario, Nelly. 2007. "Feasting on *Sancocho* before Night Falls: A Meditation." *Callaloo* 30(1): 259–81.

Rout, Leslie B., Jr. 1976. *The African Experience in Latin America*. Cambridge: Cambridge University Press.

Russell, Kathy, Midge Wilson, and Ronald Hall. 1992. *The Color Complex: The Politics of Skin Color among African Americans*. New York: Harcourt Brace Jovanovich, Publishers.

Safa, Helen I. 2005. "Challenging Mestizaje." *Critique of Anthropology* 25(3): 307–30.

———. 1998. "Introduction." *Latin American Perspectives: Race and National Identity in the Americas* 25(3): 3–20.

Sagás, Ernesto. 2000. *Race and Politics in the Dominican Republic*. Gainesville: University Press of Florida.

San Miguel, Pedro L. 2006. *The Imagined Island: History, Identity, and Utopia in Hispaniola*. Chapel Hill: University of North Carolina Press.

Segal, Daniel. 1993. "'Race' and 'Colour' in Pre-Independence Trinidad and Tobago." In *Trinidad Ethnicity*, ed. Kevin Yelvington, 81–115. Knoxville: University of Tennessee Press, 81–115.

Silié, Rubén. 1976. *Economía, Esclavitud y Población*. Santo Domingo: Universidad Autónoma de Santo Domingo.

Simmel, Georg. 1950. "The Stranger." In *The Sociology of Georg Simmel*, ed. Kurt H. Wolff, 401–8. Glencoe: The Free Press.

Simmons, Kimberly Eison. 2008. "Navigating the Racial Terrain: Blackness and Mixedness in the United States and the Dominican Republic." *Transforming Anthropology* 16(2): 95–111.

———. 2006. "Racial Enculturation and Lived Experience: Reflections on Race at Home and Abroad." *Anthropology News* 47(2): 10–11.

———. 2005. "'Somos una Liga': Afro-Dominicanidad and the Articulation of New Racial Identities in the Dominican Republic." *Wadabagei* 8(1): 51–64.

———. 2001. "A Passion for Sameness: Encountering a Black Feminist Self in Fieldwork in the Dominican Republic." In *Black Feminist Anthropology: Theory, Politics, Praxis, and Poetics*, ed. Irma McClaurin, 77–101. New Brunswick, N.J.: Rutgers University Press.

Skidmore, Thomas. 2003. "Racial Mixture and Affirmative Action: The Cases of Brazil and the United States." *American Historical Review* (December): 1391–96.

Smedley, Audrey. 1993. *Race in North America: Origin and Evolution of a Worldview*. Boulder, Colo.: Westview Press.

Tejada Ortiz, Dagoberto. 1998. *Cultura Popular e Identidad Nacional*. Santo Domingo: Mediabyte, S.A.

Thomas, Deborah. 2004. *Modern Blackness: Nationalism, Globalization, and the Politics of Culture in Jamaica*. Durham, N.C.: Duke University Press.

Torres, Arlene. 1998. "La Gran Familia Puertorriqueña 'Ej Prieta De Beldá' (The Great Puerto Rican Family Is Really Black)." In *Blackness in Latin America and the Caribbean*, ed. Norman E. Whitten and Arlene Torres, 2: 285–306. Bloomington: Indiana University Press.

Torres-Saillant, Silvio. 2006. "Blackness and Meaning in Hispaniola: A Review Essay." *Small Axe: A Caribbean Journal of Criticism* 19: 180–88.

———. 2000. "The Tribulation of Blackness: Stages of Dominican Racial Identity." *Callaloo* 23(3): 1086–1111.

———. 1995. "The Dominican Republic." In *No Longer Invisible: Afro-Latin Americans Today*, ed. Minority Rights Group, 109–38. London: Minority Rights Publications.

Torres-Saillant, Silvio, and Ramona Hernández. 1998. *The Dominican Americans.* Westport, Conn.: Greenwood Press.

Turits, Richard Lee. 2002. "A World Destroyed, a Nation Imposed: The 1937 Haitian Massacre in the Dominican Republic." *Hispanic American Historical Review* 82(3): 589–635.

Twine, Frances Windance. 1998. *Racism in a Racial Democracy: The Maintenance of White Supremacy in Brazil.* New Brunswick, N.J.: Rutgers University Press.

Vega, Bernardo. 1986. *La Vida Cotidiana Dominicana: A Traves del Archivo Particular del Generalisimo.* Santo Domingo: Fundación Cultural Dominicana.

Vega, Bernardo, Carlos Dobal, Carlos Esteban Deive, Rubén Silié, José del Castillo, and Frank Moya Pons. 1997. *Ensayos sobre Cultura Dominicana.* Santo Domingo: Amigo del Hogar.

Vicioso, Sherezada. 2000. "Dominicanyorkness: A Metropolitan Discovery of the Triangle." Trans. Daisy Cocco-DeFilippis. *Callaloo* 23(3): 1013–16.

Vizcarrondo, Fortunato. [1942] 1968. *Dinga y mandinga.* San Juan: Instituto de Cultura Puertorriqueña.

Wade, Peter. 1997. *Race and Ethnicity in Latin America.* Chicago: Pluto Press.

———. 1993. *Blackness and Race Mixture: The Dynamics of Racial Identity in Colombia.* Baltimore: Johns Hopkins University Press.

Waters, Mary. 1999. *Black Identities: West Indian Immigrant Dreams and American Realities.* Cambridge, Mass.: Harvard University Press.

Whitten, Norman E., and Arlene Torres. 1998. *Blackness in Latin America and the Caribbean.* Vols. 1 and 2. Bloomington: Indiana University Press.

Williams, Brackette F. 1989. "A Class Act: Anthropology and the Race to Nation across Ethnic Terrain." *Annual Review of Anthropology* 18: 401–44.

Williams, Eric. 1970. *From Columbus to Castro: The History of the Caribbean 1492–1969.* New York: Harper and Row Publishers.

Winn, Peter. 1992. "A Question of Color." In *Americas: The Changing Face of Latin America and the Caribbean*, 277–306. Berkeley: University of California Press.

Wright, Winthrop. 1990. *Café con Leche: Race, Class, and National Image in Venezuela.* Austin: University of Texas Press.

Yelvington, Kevin. 2001. "The Anthropology of Afro-Latin America and the Caribbean: Diasporic Dimensions." *Annual Review of Anthropology* 30(1): 227–60.

Záiter Mejía, Alba Josefina. 1996. *La Identidad Social y Nacional en Dominicana: Un Análisis Psico-Social*. Santo Domingo: Editora Taller.

Newspapers and Magazines

Ebony, Chicago
Essence, New York
El Diario, Santiago, Dominican Republic (1930)
Listin Diario, Santo Domingo, Dominican Republic
El Siglo, Santiago, Dominican Republic

Website Addresses

http://centroespanol.com/fotos-del-pasado.html
http://pdba.georgetown.edu/Elecdata/DomRep/drpr196.html
http://www.centroleon.org.do

Index

Africa, 1, 4, 27, 95, 105, 107, 109

African Americans, 2–4, 10–13, 70–72, 74, 77–78, 84–85, 87–88; and color, 4; hair, 2–4; middle-class, 2. *See also* Black Americans

African Americans and Dominicans. *See* Dominicans and African Americans

African American students, 10, 50, 69–70, 82–84, 86

African descent, 4, 17, 28, 78, 96, 102, 112

African Diaspora, 12–16, 66–69, 71, 78, 90–91, 98–99, 114–15

Africanidad, 11–13, 15–16, 33–34, 90–91, 97–99, 107, 118–20

African past, 1, 3–5, 13–16, 78, 89, 113–15, 119–20; and African ancestry, 1–2, 13, 16, 36–37, 58–59, 98–99, 103; burying the past, 1–13; unburying the past, 115–20

Africans, 1, 16–17, 19–20, 28, 67, 93, 101; Africans and Native Americans, 19

Afro-Dominican, 13, 48, 59, 66, 89–91, 97–99, 101–3; and identity, 91, 98–99, 100, 102, 104, 118

Afro-Dominicanness, 85, 89, 114, 134

Afro-Venezuelans, 59, 112–13

ALARA (Afro-Latin American Research Association), 92

Alvarez, Julia, 2, 74

Anti-Haitianism, 21, 28–29

Aparicio, Ana, 66, 81

Arrival Story, 5–9

Black Americans, 21, 72, 91. *See also* African Americans

Black community, 6, 17, 70, 72, 87, 92, 96

Black consciousness, 88–89

Black denial, 1–2, 4–5, 115

Blackening and whitening and ideas of mixture, 13, 61, 65, 67, 69, 71, 75

Black ethnic groups, 78, 96

Blackface, 112

Blackness, 2, 4–5, 10–11, 34, 70–71, 87, 113–16; constructed vis-à-vis Haitians, 4; denied by the state, 5; Dominican blackness in the United States, 87–89; and tourism, 111–12; in the United States and the Dominican Republic (comparative), 10–12

Blanco, 22, 24, 29–30, 36–38, 45–49, 55–56, 117; mixture of, 38, 55; and women (*blanca*), 31, 37, 46, 51, 57

Blanqueamiento, 12, 18, 27–28, 32

Candelario, Ginetta, 1–2, 4, 15, 46, 66, 81, 84

Caribbean, 19–20, 24, 62, 68, 91–94, 105, 120; Hispanic Caribbean, 6, 16–17, 66, 68, 119

Catholic Church, 21, 114

Cédula (national identification card), 11–13, 15–17, 33–37, 39–40, 42–51, 58, 78–79; application process, 45; new, 34–36, 43–49; and color categories, 49; issuance process (cedulazation), 43–51

Census, 12, 15–18, 21–29, 31–32, 36, 40, 43

Centro Español, 30–31

CIEE (Council on International Educational Exchange/Council Study Center), 6, 69, 82–83

Cimarrona (Identidad's newsletter), 109

Citizenship, 7, 42, 82–83

Color, 22–23, 25–26, 31–32, 34–43, 45–59, 86–90, 116–19; color categories, 5, 11, 16–17, 26, 37, 40–41, 44–46; compared to Puerto Ricans, 64; dark-skinned, 17, 96; dark-skinned and African American, 4, 50, 82; dark-skinned and Dominican, 8, 10, 18; dark-skinned and Haitian, 39; dark-skinned as *indio oscuro*, 28; dark-skinned as *negro*, 10; and identities, 52, 54, 57, 59; light-skinned, 86–87, 102; light-skinned and African American, 6–7, 17, 50; light-skinned and Dominican, 20, 22, 26, 64; light-skinned as *indio claro*, 28; prevalent color category, 16; and social class, 107

Kimberly Eison Simmons, president of the Association of Black Anthropologists, is an assistant professor of anthropology and African American studies at the University of South Carolina. She is a contributor to *Routes of Passage: Rethinking the African Diaspora* (Michigan State, 2007), *La Ruta del Esclavo* (Editora Búho, 2006), and *Black Feminist Anthropology* (Rutgers, 2001).